GLOBALIZATION, GENDER, AND PEACEBUILDING

The Future of Interfaith Dialogue

KWOK PUI-LAN

2011 Madeleva Lecture in Spirituality

Paulist Press
New York/Mahwah, NJ

Book and cover design by Lynn Else

Library of Congress Cataloging-in-Publication Data

Kwok, Pui-lan.
    Globalization, gender, and peacebuilding : the future of interfaith dialogue / Kwok Pui-lan.
        p. cm.
    "2011 Madeleva lecture in spirituality."
    Includes bibliographical references (p.   ).
    ISBN 978-0-8091-4772-4 (alk. paper)
    1. Religions—Relations. 2. Globalization—Religious aspects. 3. Women and religion. 4. Peace-building—Religious aspects. I. Title.
    BL410.K96 2012
    201′.5—dc23
                                                            2011043511

Published by Paulist Press
997 Macarthur Boulevard
Mahwah, New Jersey 07430

www.paulistpress.com

Printed and bound in the
United States of America

Globalization Gender, and Peacebuilding GLOBAL-
IZATION, GENDER, AND PEACEBUILDING **Global-
ization, Gender, and Peacebuilding** Globalization,
Gender and Peacebuilding GLOBALIZATION,
GENDER, AND PEACEBUILDING **Globalization,
Gender, and Peacebuilding** Globalization, Gender
and Peacebuilding GLOBALIZATION, GENDER, AND
PEACEBUILDING **Globalization, Gender, and Peace-
building** Globalization, Gender and Peacebuilding
GLOBALIZATION, GENDER, AND PEACEBUILDING
Globalization, Gender, and Peacebuilding Global-
ization, Gender and Peacebuilding GLOBALIZATION,
GENDER, AND PEACEBUILDING **Globalization,
Gender, and Peacebuilding** Globalization, Gender
and Peacebuilding GLOBALIZATION, GENDER, AND
PEACEBUILDING **Globalization, Gender, and
Peacebuilding** Globalization, Gender and Peace-
building GLOBALIZATION, GENDER, AND PEACE-
BUILDING **Globalization, Gender, and Peace-
building** Globalization, Gender and Peacebuilding
GLOBALIZATION, GENDER, AND PEACEBUILDING
Globalization, Gender, and Peacebuilding
Globalization, Gender and Peacebuilding GLOBALI-
ZATION, GENDER, AND PEACEBUILDING **Globaliza-
tion, Gender, and Peace- building** Globalization,
Gender and Peacebuilding GLOBALIZATION,
GENDER, AND PEACEBUILDING **Globalization,
Gender, and Peacebuilding** Globalization, Gender
and Peacebuilding GLOBALIZATION, GENDER, AND

CONTENTS

Kwok Pui-lan is the William F. Cole Professor of Christian Theology and Spirituality at the Episcopal Divinity School in Cambridge, Massachusetts. She was president of the American Academy of Religion in 2011 and has published extensively in the areas of Asian feminist theology, biblical interpretation, and postcolonial criticism. An internationally known theologian, she received her doctorate from Harvard University. Dr. Kwok is the author of *Postcolonial Imagination and Feminist Theology* (2005); *Introducing Asian Feminist Theology* (2000); and *Discovering the Bible in the Non-Biblical World* (1995). She is the coeditor of *Empire and the Christian Tradition: New Readings of Classical Theologians* (2007); and *Off the Menu: Asian and Asian North American Women's Religion and Theology* (2007). Dr. Kwok is also the editor of the major reference work *Women and Christianity*, 4 volumes (2010); and *Hope Abundant: Third World and Indigenous Women's Theology* (2010).

INTRODUCTION

In January of 2011, the demonstrations and protests in Tunisia led to the ouster of president and strongman Zine el-Abidine Ben Ali. The peaceful demonstrations in Cairo's Tahrir Square in February captured worldwide attention and led to the downfall of the regime of Egyptian President Hosni Mubarak and his subsequent trial. The wave of political uprising soon swept across the Arab world, as protesters in the Middle East and North Africa took to the streets to demand radical reforms and social changes. In some countries, such as Libya, Syria, and Yemen, the people's aspirations for democracy have been met with violent suppression.

The series of protests has been called the "Arab spring" or "Arab awakening," even though not all of the participants are Arab. The revolutionary ferment to create more open and democratic societies has changed some people's perceptions and stereotypical images of people in the Muslim world, for, ever since September 11, 2001, and the war on terrorism, conservative politicians and right-wing pundits have tried to link Islam with terrorism and violence.

Religion has played an enormous role in contemporary politics and in the discussions of war and peace, identity and tradition, authoritarianism and democracy. In the United States, the proposal to establish a mosque near Ground Zero, where the twin towers of the World Trade Center were attacked, unleashed acrimonious arguments for months. In Norway, the massacre of innocent people by far-right, Islamphobic Anders Behring Breivik in the summer of 2011 shocked this country, which has been proud of its inclusivity and tolerance.

Religion has had a resurgence in many parts of the world and has entered the public domain and policy discussions, both nationally and internationally. There is clearly a change of attitude in the secular state and in public discourse with respect to the enduring impulses of religion and religious communities. Some have called this the postsecular world. If Max Weber associated the disenchantment of the world with the rise of capitalism and modernity, today scholars in religion are busy exploring the reasons for the "permanence" of the theologico-political.[1]

In our contemporary world, globalization and the mass media have spawned a secular and consumerist culture on the one hand, and stimulated an interest in the search for cultural and religious identity on the other. Religious fundamentalism of all kinds—including Christian, Islamic, Jewish, and Hindu—can be seen in different parts of the world. In the United States, for example, the Christian Right has a strong influence in politics and exerts great pressure to steer the country toward conservative values.

Much of the debate on the significance and value of religion has been occasioned by the theory of "the clash of civilizations" proposed by the late Harvard political scientist Samuel P. Huntington.[2] In a sweeping fashion, he suggested that the future clashes of the world would not be so much influenced by ideology as by what he called civilizational differences. He opined that renewed conflicts and violence would take place between countries and cultures that base their traditions on religion and dogma.

Many critics have challenged Huntington's oversimplistic characterization of civilizations and his rigid and fixed conception of religious and cultural boundaries. But his work stimulates us to think of ways in which we can live together across religious differences and the cultural divide to create a better world for the future. For example, Huntington's former colleague at Harvard, Chinese philosopher Tu Weiming, states, "Our awareness of the danger of civilizational conflicts, rooted in ethnicity, language, land, and religion, makes the necessity of dialogue particularly appealing. An alternative model of sustainable development, with an emphasis on the ethical and spiritual dimensions of human flourishing must be sought."[3]

This book is divided into three chapters. Chapter 1 discusses how globalization has impacted interreligious relationships and dialogue. The chapter includes an account of the trajectories of interfaith dialogue in the Protestant and Catholic churches to provide a background for the discussion in subsequent chapters. The future of interfaith dialogue must include those marginalized voices that have not been invited to the table. Women have been sidelined in official events on dialogue, and many writers on theologies of religions have neglected the gender dimension. In chapter 2, I focus on gender and interfaith dialogue, exploring concerns that have been raised by women, such as Orientialist construction of religious difference, reciprocity and misappropriation, and multiple identities and hybridity. The last chapter argues that peacebuilding should be a central focus for future interfaith dialogue. I explore the concept of polydoxy, which goes beyond the logic of the One to embrace multiplicity and relationality. The remembrance of the tenth anniversary of September 11, 2001, motivates us to renew our efforts toward fostering interreligious solidarity and working for peace.

1

GLOBALIZATION, RELIGIOUS PLURALISM, AND DIALOGUE

During the Arab uprising in the spring of 2011, stories and images of demonstrations spread across the Internet through Facebook, Twitter feeds, live blogs, videos, and photos. The world could follow instantly the latest development of the protests. The rapid rise of the social media, together with traditional and digital media, connects people living in faraway lands instantly in what has been called the "global village." The term *globalization* gained currency in the 1990s at the end of the Cold War because the former demarcations of the First, Second, and Third Worlds became outdated. With the collapse of the former Soviet Union and the realignment of the Eastern European bloc, some people believed that capitalism and the neo-liberal market would dictate the world. Others believed that globalization is modernity accelerated and raised to a higher level. Globalization signifies the global reach of capitalism, the fast flows of capital and people, free trade, and the breaking down of national boundaries. The effects of globalization are hotly debated. Some scholars have offered the criticism that globalization is not new, but a continuation of Western neocolonialism in more concerted form. Yet others have also pointed out that globalization is not limited to the economic realm, but has social, cultural, and political dimensions. Globalization also has benign effects, such as the promotion of transnational grassroots movements, democracy and human rights, and the protection of biodiversity and the environment.[4]

If globalization is a compression of time and space, it not only brings people to closer proximity than before, but also heightens the immense cultural, religious, linguistic, racial, and ethnic diversities in the world. What are the impacts of globalization on religion and religious communities? According to Thomas Banchoff, a professor specializing in religious and ethical issues in world politics, religion has long had a transnational dimension. He writes, "Major world religions have grown and changed as they have spread across borders, generating far-flung networks with varied regional and local expressions."[5] He cites as examples the migration of Buddhism out of India to the various Asian countries and the reach of Islam and Christianity to huge populations of the world. The interaction of religion with world affairs is also not new. Religious beliefs and practices have implications for morality and ethics, the quest for common good, and the rightful exercise of power. The close relation between religion and politics continues into the modern imperial era.

Yet, globalization does bring in something new, Banchoff argues. Modern communications technology and near-instantaneous worldwide connections strengthen transnational religious networks and diaspora communities.[6] Even the pope got on Twitter on an Apple iPad in June 2011. Evangelical Christianity has long used mass media to cultivate its influences and to spread its individualistic understanding of the Gospel. In countries in Latin America, Africa, and Asia, religious pundits have successfully used radio and television to promulgate a "Gospel of Prosperity" and American-style consumerism. In Islam, social media and inexpensive communications allow people to form virtual communities, create transnational identities, and contest traditional and hierarchical authorities. Modern communications technology leads to the internal diversification of religious traditions because it expands the cultural and social space for religious engagement both nationally and internationally.

Instant contact with a much more complicated world than before prompts many people to question their social reality, including religious authority and institutions. Many people in the West, especially the young, declare that they are "spiritual but not religious." While mainline religious communities may be declining, new forms of expression, such as the Emergent Church within Christianity, and other new religious movements are on the rise and spreading. Religious groups form coalitions and alliances, sometimes within their religious structure and sometimes with secular groups, to address issues such as poverty, HIV/AIDS, nuclear power, and environmental concerns. Globalization and transnational linkages promote "a high level of internal diversity and the reformulation of religious identities and ethical commitments at a global level," Banchoff notes.[7]

The Debate on Religious Pluralism

Given the enormous influence religion has in world politics in our global age, how can people of different religious backgrounds and commitments live and work peacefully together? In multireligious and multicultural Asia, people of different religious traditions have lived side by side with one another for millennia. In China, for example, Buddhist and Daoist influences contributed to the rise of Neo-Confucian philosophy in the tenth to the thirteenth centuries. In India, a land of ancient civilizations, Hindus, Muslims, Christians, and people of other traditions interacted and coexisted, sometimes peacefully and sometimes entering into conflicts, as we have seen in recent times.

But in Europe and North America, Christianity has been the dominating religious tradition, and the church has had a strong exclusive claim to truth and authority. Immigration in the last several decades and transnational movements of people have changed the religious landscape in the United States and some European countries. Religious diversity in Western countries increasingly mirrors religious diversity in the world as a whole. This change has precipitated tremendous anxiety and pointed debates related to national identity, cultural heritage, and the integration of immigrants into a growing heterogeneous society. The explosive nature of the debates is evident in the aftermath of the depictions of Prophet Mohammed in a Danish newspaper and after the massacre of innocents by Norwegian Anders Behring Breivik. A closer examination of how religion is understood and religious boundaries have been constructed in the West is in order.

Religion is a contested term, and scholars have long debated what it means. Some scholars trace it to the Latin *relego*, meaning "to read again" or "repeat" as one engages scripture and creeds. Others argue that it comes from the Latin word *religare*, "to bind anew" as in a covenant or contract; still others insist that the origin can be traced to the Latin *res-legere*, "with regard to a gathering." The term was not used frequently until the Enlightenment, when the need arose to differentiate the religious from the secular. In its modern usage, *religion* often connotes a set of religious beliefs and an institutionalized community. Mark Juergensmeyer writes, "It is used to demarcate the ideas, practices, beliefs, and institutions that are related to a particular faith and tradition that has a name—such as Christianity—and can be labeled as a religion."[8] As a scholar who has done field research on the religion of Untouchables in Punjab, India, Juergensmeyer hastens to add that the word *religion* cannot be easily translated into non-European languages because of different cultural constructs.

Christianity arose as a small movement persecuted by the Roman Empire and struggled to exist among people following Greek, Roman, and Jewish religious traditions. Many Christians died as martyrs because their religious values conflicted with social and imperial power. With the conversion of Constantine and the Edict of Milan in 313 CE, Christianity became the dominant religion of the Empire, and the suppression of other religious traditions followed. Facing the threats of so-called schismatics and heretics in the third century, Cyprian, the bishop of Carthage (d. 258), sought to bolster the authority of bishops and the church by arguing that there could be no salvation for anyone except in the church. Originally meant for persons already in the church as a warning, Cyprian's proclamation was directed at non-Christians after the fifth century and through the

Middle Ages.[9] The central Christian axiom *extra ecclesiam, nulla salus* (outside the church, no salvation) became the official teaching, reiterated and further developed by popes and councils. In 1215 Pope Innocent III and the Fourth Lateran Council stated, "There is one universal church of the faithful, outside of which no one at all is saved." The Council of Florence in 1442 made the relation between the church and people who worshipped other faiths more explicit:

[The Holy Roman Church] firmly believes, professes and teaches that none of those who exist outside the Catholic Church—neither pagans nor Jews nor heretics nor schismatics —can become sharers of eternal life; rather they will go into the eternal fire "which was prepared for the devil and his angels" (Matt. 25:42).[10]

In the religious construction of fifteenth-century Europe, there were Christians, Jews, Muslims, and all others called pagans who followed the traditions of the Greeks and Romans. During the fifteenth to seventeenth centuries, the need to differentiate Christianity from other traditions gave rise to the imagination of "other religions" and the "religious others." Christianity as a label appeared in polemical literature in the sixteenth century; Judaism, Mahometanism [*sic*], and Paganism, as labels for these traditions, arrived in the first half of the seventeenth century. As a result of the Catholic Reformation, missionaries, especially the Jesuits, were sent to East Asia and the Americas. They brought back knowledge of cultures, customs, and religious traditions from these distant lands. The encounter of the wide variety of civilizations and cultures because of the missionary movement and colonization necessitated the reclassification of religion. In the nineteenth century, Hinduism, Buddhism, and Daoism were recognized as "world religions."[11] Compared with Christianity, these religions were considered superstitious and heathen, often cast in negative light. Indigenous and oral traditions in Africa and the Americas were either not recognized as religion or dubbed as primitive religion. In her book *The Invention of World Religions*, Tomoko Masuzawa remarks that this new discourse of diversity of religions in the first half of the nineteenth century "neither displaced nor disabled the logic of European hegemony—formerly couched in the language of the universality of Christianity—but, in a way, gave it a new lease."[12]

In the United States, Protestantism, Catholicism, and Judaism were considered the three major traditions till the mid-twentieth century. The Immigration Act of 1965 lifted the national origins quota system and allowed people from different parts of the world to immigrate to the States.

The influx of new immigrants and the religious communities they have formed have drastically reshaped the American religious landscape. In *A New Religious America*, Diana Eck of Harvard University has argued that the United States has changed from a "Christian country" to become the world's most religiously diverse nation.[13] She and her colleagues at the Pluralism Project at Harvard have done ethnographical and other studies to document the implosion of non-Christian religions, the contours of the American multireligious society, the interaction between different religious groups, and the impacts on civic life.[14]

Take, for example, the city of Los Angeles. It can boast of being the most religiously diverse city in the world. There are 131 Buddhist temples and meditation centers, fifty-eight mosques, eighteen Hindu temples, and sixteen Shinto worship centers in Los Angeles County.[15] In the debate on building the mosque near Ground Zero, people might have easily forgotten that mosques have been part of New York's architectural and religious mix for over a century. From ten mosques in New York in 1970, the number has grown to more than one hundred, and seventeen in Manhattan alone. Some 800,000 of the 8.21 million residents in the city are Muslims, many whose New York roots go back generations. Like the Catholic and Jewish immigrants who came before them, the

Muslims in New York seek to be part of the city and the country.[16]

The changing religious landscape in America requires us to rethink relations and interactions among the different religious groups and communities. Instead of the exclusivist model, which closes its door to foreigners and aliens, such as the Chinese Exclusion Act of 1882, and the assimilationist model, which touts America as the "melting pot," the model of religious pluralism has gained popularity in the past decades. I focus on Diana Eck since the Pluralism Project is one of the best-known and influential forums of researchers and networks. Diana Eck offers the following four points to consider the meaning of pluralism. First, she distinguishes between diversity and pluralism. Diversity means plurality, and different religious groups or worship centers can exist in the same neighborhood without engagement or relationship. Pluralism is not diversity alone, but "the energetic engagement with diversity." Second, pluralism goes beyond tolerance, which is a thin foundation for interaction and engagement. Instead, pluralism is "the active seeking of understanding across lines of difference." Third, pluralism is not relativism, accepting different approaches as equally valid without discrimination, but "the encounter of commitments." One does not need to give up one's religious identity or values, but must hold religious difference, not in isolation, but in

14

relationship to one another. Finally, pluralism is "based on dialogue," seeking to identify commonalities and real differences, and in the process there is give and take, listening as well as speaking.[17]

Although the pluralistic model seems to be better able to address religious difference than the exclusive and assimilationist models, it has its severe critics. For conservative Christians, whose influence in American society is gaining momentum, the pluralistic model risks giving up Christian uniqueness and the claim that Christianity is the true religion. In addition to conservative Christians, some scholars also have misgivings about pluralism and point to its political and ideological underpinnings. For example, British theologian John Milbank has argued that pluralism is rooted in Western modernity and associated with Enlightenment ideas. Immanuel Kant and other Enlightenment philosophers have argued for subjecting all religion to the court of universal reason. Religion is largely treated as a private affair, and all religions are treated as equal by the secular nation-state. Under the rule of universal reason, the particularity of religious traditions and alternative cultural visions are eclipsed. For Milbank, pluralism is a rhetoric to avoid real difference and, as a consequence, the celebration of different cultures and traditions is actually "the obliteration of other cultures by western norms and categories, with their freight of Christian influence."[18] Others find that pluralism is based on "repressive tolerance," a characteristic of Western liberalism, and does not really promote engagement across difference.[19] Stanley Hauerwas even calls for an "end of religious pluralism" and writes:

> From my perspective, pluralism is the ideology used by Protestant liberals to give themselves the illusion they are still in control of, or at least have responsibility for, the future of America. Religion is the designation created to privatize strong convictions in order to render them harmless so that alleged democracies can continue to have the illusion they flourish on difference.[20]

Both Milbank and Hauerwas have argued for clearer articulation of religious difference, an affirmation of Christian particularity, and a return to central Christian narratives and doctrines to resist the encroachment of the secular and liberal modernity. Milbank is a key proponent of the theological movement called Radical Orthodoxy, which criticizes atheistic and nihilistic secularism and uses the tools of postmodern philosophy to challenge major tenets of modernity.

In the twenty-first century, the old idea of "religion" may change, the invention of "world religions" has been under serious scrutiny, and religious pluralism is hotly contested in the United

States and abroad. Our global age enables both new cultural creations, the refashioning of religious identity and relationships, and the internal diversification of religious traditions. How will all these impact the future of interfaith dialogue? I begin with a discussion of the trajectories of dialogue in the Christian tradition.

Trajectories of Interfaith Dialogue

After the Second World War, when the colonial powers collapsed and new nations came into being, the Christian church faced a new reality in which formerly colonized peoples demanded their cultural autonomy and recognition. As Raimon Panikkar notes, dialogue becomes "the new catchword after the dismantling of the colonial political order. There is a trend now toward indigenization, inculturation, greater respect for other religions, and attempts at a new interpretation of the christic fact."[21] In some quarters, the term *interfaith dialogue* is used instead of interreligious dialogue to signal that conversations and interactions are taking place between people of faiths, and not between religions per se, between religions as systems of beliefs and practices. Conferences, books, and church documents on dialogue proliferate. Dialogue is happening on many levels: among religious leaders in ecumenical gatherings, scholars in academic venues, and at the local congregations and grassroots.

As we look back to the past century, we can see that dialogue has been conceptualized in very different terms under changing historical circumstances. In the early half of the twentieth century, church mission was the primary focus and dialogue was subordinate to it. This was most evident at the World Missionary Conference in Edinburgh in 1910. Attended by 1,200 delegates, the Edinburgh gathering was orchestrated by the charismatic American John R. Mott, who popularized the missionary slogan of "Evangelization of the world in this generation." Among its eight commissions, Commission Four discussed and issued a report on "Missionary Message in Relation to the Non-Christian World." The report exhorts Christians to treat other religions with respect and sympathy, and their adherents as fellow pilgrims. Yet, the report is clearly missiological in its tone. Even as Christians were encouraged to learn from other believers, they were also charged to bear witness to the Christian faith.

Knowledge about other religions and good relations with non-Christians would certainly facilitate Christian mission understood as evangelism. Peter C. Phan argues that although the Edinburgh Conference did not use the terms *interreligious* or *interfaith dialogue*, and Christians conversed among themselves and not with other religious adherents, the conference encouraged what we would call dialogue today.[22] The conference adopted what would be later called "fulfillment theology," believing that Jesus has not come "to abolish, but to fulfill" (Matt 5:17). Although other religious traditions may have positive elements, they are deficient by themselves and only prepare for the final fulfillment in Jesus Christ.

About fifty years later, Vatican II (1962–65) signaled a new, radical departure in terms of Catholic teachings on non-Christian religions. Compared to the "outside the church, no salvation" posture, Vatican II was much more conciliatory in tone with a much more positive attitude toward other religions. The Declaration on the Relationship of the Church to the Non-Christian Religions (*Nostra Aetate*) states that God's love is not limited to the walls of the church. It makes positive references and comments about other religious traditions and applauds the "profound religious sense" found in them. It affirms that their teachings and practices "reflect a ray of the Truth that enlightens all peoples," and most importantly it exhorts all Catholics to "dialogue and collaborate" with other believers and so "in witness of Christian faith and life, to acknowledge, preserve, and promote the spiritual and moral goods found among these people" (*Nostra Aetate* 2).

Phan points out that Vatican II offered teachings on mission and interreligious dialogue almost identical to those of the Edinburgh Conference, even though the council did not make reference to it. Like Edinburgh, Vatican II issued an urgent call to mission and saw church mission as a prolongation of the mission of God (*missio Dei*). The Decree on the Church's Missionary Activity states, "Missionary activity is nothing else, and nothing less, than the manifestation of God's plan, its epiphany and realization in the world and in history; that by which God, through mission, clearly brings to its conclusion the history of salvation" (*Ad Gentes* 9). Though the council recognized elements of truth and grace in other religions, it reiterated the central importance of Christ as the universal savior. The mission of the church is to bring non-Christians to Christ, for "whatever good or truth is found amongst them [non-Christians], is considered by the church to be a preparation for the Gospel" (*Lumen Gentium* 16). Thus, similar to Edinburgh, Vatican II also regarded Christianity as the fulfillment of other religions and dialogue as part of the church's evangelistic mission.

In the 1960s and 1970s, activities related to dialogue began to gain momentum both in the Catholic and Protestant churches. After Vatican II, the Secretariat on Non-Christians was created, now renamed the Pontifical Council for Interreligious Dialogue. In 1970, the Central Committee of the World Council of Churches (WCC) declared interreligious dialogue as "the common pilgrimage of the churches," and the WCC published *Guidelines on Dialogue*. The WCC created in 1971 a subunit called Dialogue of People of Living Faiths and Ideologies, which facilitated encounters with religious leaders of other traditions and invited Christian communities with long experience of life in pluralistic contexts to share their experience.[23] The current WCC program on Interreligious Dialogue and Cooperation continues the work. Today interfaith dialogue is not only discussed by Christian bodies, but is on the agenda of Muslim, Jewish, Hindu, and Buddhist organizations.

Interfaith dialogue gradually began to be separated from mission and evangelism, with its own distinct focus and tasks. Part of the reason is that the missionary movement has been criticized as a tool of cultural imperialism, serving colonial expansion. Thus, interfaith dialogue should not aim to convert or proselytize with the assumption that Christianity is superior to other religions. A report of the 1970 WCC consultation on dialogue, which brought Hindus, Buddhists, Muslims, and Christians together for the first time under the auspices of the WCC, spells out clearly this new understanding of dialogue. Dialogue is the meeting between people of living faiths, and not between Christianity and other religions. Each one is speaking as a person of faith out of deep and firm commitment to his or her faith and tradition. Each one must come to dialogue with openness and frankness, ready to learn from one another in a spirit of mutuality and reciprocity. Only so can dialogue foster mutual understanding and help to overcome biases, preconceived notions, and prejudices. People of all faiths have common responsibility toward today's social and political problems. Dialogue helps to identify common concerns and promote the building of wider human community. Finally, dialogue should not be confined to the academic level, but should take place at all levels of society.[24]

Since Vatican II, the Catholic Church has engaged in sustained reflection on dialogue and religious plurality within itself and with leaders and scholars of other religious traditions. The 1991 document "Dialogue and Proclamation" articulates four forms of dialogue.[25] The dialogue of life takes place in our interaction with our neighbors, and in our families, communities, and workplaces. Given the increased religious diversity in America, we will meet people of different faiths and ethnicities in our schools, our town halls, and in our social and religious functions. The dialogue of action happens when people and religious organizations of different faith traditions collaborate and work together to address shared problems of a local community or wider concerns. Such action may take different forms, such as witnessing to the structural and social manifestations of injustice, political advocacy for policy changes, and caring for the poor through feeding programs and food pantries. The dialogue of spiritual experience may involve interreligious sharing of rituals, worship, prayers, celebrations, meditations, or civic liturgy. For Christians, it is not incorporating other religious elements into our worship or interpreting other religious symbols and rituals through our lens. Rather, it is experiencing a spiritual practice with others and understanding the meaning of it in its particular tradition to arrive at deeper understanding. The greatest challenge is the dialogue of beliefs, dogma, and theology. Different traditions have their normative claims, and religious doctrines and dogmas are embedded in particular cultural frames and religious worldviews. How do we understand each other when religious concepts and terminologies often defy translation? How can we speak about our religious beliefs with integrity, while accepting the validity of the truth claims of other traditions?

In the past several decades, three approaches have been identified by scholars writing in the area of theology of religions and interfaith dialogue.[26] The first is the *exclusive* stance, which believes that other religions have no value and Christianity is meant to replace them all. This approach is still found in many Christian churches, especially among the Fundamentalist or Evangelical churches.

Karl Barth also belongs to this camp, when he wrote during the Nazi period that all religion (including Christianity) is unbelief, and salvation can only be brought through Christ alone. The second is the *inclusivist* approach, which recognizes truths and values in other religions. These other traditions are leading to and in preparation for Christ and to be fulfilled in Christianity. Proponents of inclusivism stress the universality of God's love and God's plan for all to be saved. The Catholic theologian Karl Rahner is a representative of the inclusive approach: Rahner maintained that God's grace is found in other religions and famously referred to people of other faiths as "anonymous Christians." The Buddhists and Hindus who experience the grace of God in their religion are already connected with and directed toward Jesus, since Jesus is the ultimate gift of God. They are, in a sense, already Christians, even though they do not call themselves so. Rahner's new approach to other religions has influenced Vatican II and many other Catholic theologians.

The third one is the *pluralist* approach, which, as I said, has become popular among mainline and progressive theologians and scholars of religion. If the inclusivists believe that one tradition— Christianity—contains all salvific truth, the pluralists believe that all the religious traditions are valid paths to salvation. The pluralists do not speak with one voice, and they have taken philosophical, mystical, and ethical approaches to describe the encounters of religions. One of the leading proponents is John Hick, who has written many books on the subject. For Hick, God, the Divine, or the Real, is inexhaustible and infinitely beyond our grasp, and the diverse religious traditions are cultural expressions of the same reality. There is one *noumen*, but many religious phenomena. The different religions are like the diverse paths we can follow to climb a mountain, and they point to the same goals.[27] Hick's assumptions that people's religious experience is common and that believers are journeying toward the same goal have been criticized. Mark Heim, for example, argues that the differences among the religions cannot be overlooked and it is premature to say that their ultimate goals are the same. He writes, "Nirvana and communion with God are contradictory only if we assume that one or the other must be the sole fate for all human beings."[28] Instead, he proposes that there are two different endpoints and two different realities. Instead of one salvation common to all, Heim argues that there are different salvations, and the religions are moving toward different fulfillments and destinations. The world religions are not paths leading up the same religious mountain; rather, they are paths up very different mountains.

Asian churches and theologians have contributed significantly to the discussion on religious plurality and dialogue because of their long history of life in multireligious contexts. Stanley Samartha and Wesley Ariarajah have directed the WCC sub-unit on dialogue and made critical contributions to the subject. Aloysius Pieris, a Jesuit from Sri Lanka who has advanced training in both Buddhism and Christianity, urges his colleagues in the Ecumenical Association of Third World Theologians to pay attention to dialogue and not just focus on social and political liberation. For him, Asia is character-ized not only by poverty, but also by religious plu-rality. He points out that the majority of the hungry and poor people of the world are non-Christians, and we cannot achieve world peace without learn-ing their religious symbols and their visions for life, and collaborating with them in concrete action. He writes poignantly:

> The irruption of the Third World is also the irruption of the non-Christian world. The vast majority of God's poor perceive their ultimate concern and symbolize their struggle for liberation in the idiom of non-Christian religions and cultures. Therefore, a theology that does not speak to or through this non-Christian peoplehood is an esoteric luxury of a Christian minority.[29]

Another Catholic theologian who has made out-standing contributions to the literature on dialogue is Raimon Panikkar, born of an Indian Hindu father and Spanish Catholic mother. With a capacious mind and erudition, Panikkar could write in several languages and knew many different traditions. For him, interreligious dialogue must be accompanied by intrareligious dialogue, which is a kind of reflexivity, a self-questioning of one's own tradition after encountering with other traditions. He defines intrareligious dialogue as "an inner dialogue within myself, an encounter in the depth of my personal religiousness, having met another religious experience on that very intimate level."[30] In intrareligious dialogue, one begins with questioning oneself and one's beliefs to see both in a new light. If our faith is a living faith, it must be constantly renewed and demands ever-recurring *metanoia*. He uses the term *cosmotheandric experience* to describe our emerging religious consciousness, which encompasses the world, the divine, and the human. This experience dwells within and is found among various religions in the world and constitutes a mystical awareness of the unity with the divine, with all other human beings, and with creation.[31]

Whereas interreligious or interfaith dialogue describes the encounter of people of different traditions, in the 1980s, scholars began to discuss the notion of double or multiple religious belonging and participation.[32] The issue has surfaced in Confucian-Christian dialogue when Confucian participants asked if one could have dual citizenship by participating in more than one tradition at once. Participants in Hindu-Christian dialogue have also broached the same question. As North America is becoming more religiously pluralistic, some scholars argue that multiple religious participation will be increasingly common and become an issue of faith and practice. Others are more cautious for fear that multiple religious belonging would bring back the age-old issue of syncretism—the mixing of gods and religions. Judith Berling, who has studied religion in the Chinese context, suggests that the interplay of religious traditions is more dynamic and fluid in some cultures. Using the Chinese case as an example, she wants to expand the Christian horizon in looking at religious diversity and stresses the importance of hospitality in living with one's religious neighbors and in interfaith dialogue.[33]

From understanding dialogue as service to mission in the first half of the twentieth century to the discussion of multiple religious belonging, the Christian church has changed quite drastically in its attitude toward other religious traditions. As we face the future, interfaith dialogue must address some of the burning issues in our world, such as the rise of fundamentalisms of all kinds, the assertion of religious identity and fragmentation of community, the exploitation of religious passion for violence, the widespread suspicion of political and religious leaders, and cynicism about possible social change. Interfaith dialogue must be a force for peacekeeping. In contemporary politics there are the dual forces of politicization of religion and the theologization of politics. Sadly, religion is a contributing factor to conflicts and violence in some of the war-torn and poorest areas in Africa, South India, Palestine, and other parts in the Middle East. As Mark Juergensmeyer points out, violence has a shadowy presence lurking within the histories of religious traditions from biblical times to our present moment. Religion has provided the motivation, justification, organization, and worldview for public acts of violence.[34] It is therefore imperative for people of all faiths to work toward a future in which religion can be a force not for destruction but for the common good. Juergensmeyer observes: "...this historical moment of global transformation has provided an occasion for religion—with all its images and ideas—to be reasserted as a public force."[35]

If religion is to become a force of peacekeeping and not a cause for intolerance and conflict, new construction of and relations with the "religious other" must be sought. As we have seen, in the history of the West, the idea of the religious other, whether labeled as "pagans," "infidels," or "heathens," has been used as a foil to bolster Christian identity and European hegemony. The discovery of the religious other went hand-in-hand with

Europe's encounter with other parts of the world. The world religions of Islam, Hinduism, Buddhism, and Confucianism are mapped onto distant geography and strange lands, in which people live with superstition and bizarre customs. The grouping of huge populations under a single religious identity with identifiable characteristics made the management of religious difference easier for colonial control. Interfaith dialogue would benefit from insights from postcolonial studies, which questions how the self and the other, center and periphery, and cultural dominant and marginalized have been constructed.

Interfaith dialogue must not be confined to narrow academic circles and among the elites if it is going to have a wider impact on faith communities and society. In particular, those voices that have not been heard at the dialogical table must be welcome and listened to. Unfortunately, in many ecumenical gatherings and at the Parliament of the World Religions, women's participation and their voices have been marginalized. Representatives of religious traditions are mostly men, since women have not risen to high positions in many official religious hierarchies. This is unwarranted since women are an integral part of the world's religious traditions and they play pivotal roles in them. I turn now to issues related to gender and interfaith dialogue in the next chapter.

2

GENDER AND INTERFAITH DIALOGUE

Interfaith dialogue as it is practiced in different parts of the world has been dominated by men, and in the 1970s, it was even called "dialogue between men of living faiths." As we look at the events and publications on dialogue by the World Council of Churches and the Vatican, or at various gatherings of the Parliament of World Religions, we can find that gender was not an integral part of conversation. This leads Ursula King to state that feminism is a missing dimension of interfaith dialogue. King argues that feminism poses several challenges to dialogue that must be taken seriously in the future. The first is women's equal representation in events of dialogue so that women's viewpoints and experiences can be included and not be subsumed under men's. The challenge of gender is the challenge of otherness, in that a woman in dialogue might be doubly other, if she is a woman of another faith in a gathering consisting predominantly of men. In the fields of religion and theology, feminist scholars have included theoretical gender perspectives in their critical analyses. The challenge to dialogue can also be a theological one, if feminist thinkers would employ feminist insights to scrutinize the categories used in dialogue and in theology of religions.[36]

Although the official events have largely ignored them, women from different religious communities have met to share their experiences and support one another. Since the late 1960s, feminist scholars in religion have begun to examine patriarchal belief systems and religious institutions with a gender focus. Scholars at the American Academy of Religion organized the Women and Religion section to share the results of their research on women's lives in different religious traditions. At the regional and local levels, women of faith have gathered across religious, linguistic, and cultural barriers to focus on the concerns of their communities. For example, Asian women held an interfaith conference in Kuala Lumpur in 1989, bringing together Buddhist, Christian, Hindu, Jewish, and Muslim women. Participants examined oppressive and liberative aspects of their traditions, and discussed social and political discrimination against women in their contexts. They wanted to deepen their own faith in light of other traditions and foster solidarity and sisterhood by overcoming divisive barriers. In 2005, Asian feminist theologians organized a conference in a Muslim neighborhood near Bandung to commemorate the fiftieth anniversary of the Bandung Conference, a meeting of newly independent African and Asian countries. The feminist theologians chose the theme of "A Feminist Theology of Hope through Interfaith Dialogue from a Holistic Perspective." Participants discussed dialogue in the multicultural and multireligious Asian contexts and visited Muslim religious, social, and civic centers to dialogue with Muslim women leaders in the community.[37]

In the United States, Rita M. Gross, a Jewish scholar who became a devout Buddhist, observes that Western feminist theologians have not paid sufficient attention to dialogue. Having studied Buddhism and Hinduism and participated in dialogue for years, she exhorts Western women to avail themselves of the rich symbolic and spiritual resources of the East and not to limit themselves to Western sources. She values the "comparative mirror" offered through interfaith encounter and quotes Max Müller, the founder of the comparative study of religion, who said, "...to know one religion is, indeed, to know none." Gross writes, "Nothing so stimulates one's imagination about the possibilities of religion than through study of or continued dialogue with a completely different perspective."[38] The willingness to borrow a "comparative mirror" to expand one's horizon is laudatory and has been emphasized by others in interfaith dialogue. But this open-minded stance is insufficient if it fails to recognize our differential in dialogue, because women of different faiths do not enter dialogue on equal footing. Some have their tradition under severe attack by politicians and religious pundits to serve particular geopolitical purposes. We must go one further step to examine the ways race, gender, and religion, especially in the case of Islam, intersect in the construction of religious other.

Gender, Orientalism, and Religious Difference

Since September 11, 2001, the media has greatly expanded its coverage on Muslim women and women in the Arab world. Stereotypical images of Muslim women in *burqas* were repeatedly shown on television and in newspapers. Such images were meant to reinforce the notion of the antiliberal and antidemocratic stance of Muslim countries in contrast with the modern and progressive Western societies. They revitalize what Edward W. Said has called Orientalism, in which the West invariably represents the Middle East as inferior, backward, and stagnant for the sake of controlling and managing it. Said writes, "Orientalism is a style of thought based upon an ontological and epistemological distinction made between 'the Orient' and (most of the time) 'the Occident.'"[39] As Michel Foucault has said, power and knowledge go hand-in-hand; such biased representations are made possible because of unequal colonial relationships, and they in turn justify and reinforce Western hegemony.

During the war on terrorism, old colonialist and Orientalist scripts about gender and Muslim women resurfaced and have been redeployed. President George W. Bush used the religious rhetoric of "crusades" to describe his campaign against the Taliban and Al-Qaeda in Afghanistan. In the colonial days, Arab and Muslim men were depicted in Western literature as barbarous, lethargic, and dishonest, in contrast with the direct, trustworthy, and noble Anglo-Saxon men. Muslim women were cast and projected as the counterimage of the ideal Western female. They dwelled in harems and were the personification of desire. Western Orientalist paintings show them as naked or scantily clad, lounging with their slaves and eunuchs. Under the Western gaze, they are vulnerable and unhappy in their harems and need Western men to rescue them from barbarous Muslim men. Jasmin Zine, a Muslim scholar and activist in Canada, notes, "The war on terror reinvents these existing tropes and discourses in new ways that produce Muslims as dangerous foreigners, terrorists, and threats to public safety and render Muslim women as victims of their anachronistic faith, lacking agency and voice."[40]

In order to enter into dialogue with Muslim women, we must be aware of the long history of Orientalism, which has shaped scholarship as well as popular consciousness. Gender, race, and religion intersect powerfully in what Jasmin Zine has called the dual oppressions of "gender Islamophobia," because Muslim women are caught between the contradictory narratives of Orientalism and fundamentalism.[41] On the one hand, they are depicted as vulnerable and politically immature, in need of rescue and liberation through the imperialist intervention of the West. On the other hand, they are confined by gender roles prescribed by religious extremism and puritan discourses, which limit their search for human rights and freedom. In order to free themselves from religious fundamentalism and Western compassion, Muslim feminists have to contest their available scripts and renegotiate their identity and fight for their destiny.

In the fight against the Taliban, the media has widely reported the oppression of women to galvanize public support for the military campaigns. The Taliban has enforced strict gender segregation: women must wear the *burqa* in public, and they are not allowed to work or to be educated after the age of eight. People living in the West, and feminists among them, have reasons to be outraged and concerned. Yet, postcolonial critic

Gayatri Chakravorty Spivak cautions against reinscribing the colonial ideology of "white men saving brown women from brown men," which can easily be used to camouflage brutality, as if such action is called for and demanded by brown women's situation.[42] If saving brown women can mask violence and reconstitute in a blatant reversal as social mission to justify colonialism, it can also be used to justify new wars in our time. Therefore, if Western feminists are not careful of the Orientalist and racist dynamics, their compassion and agenda to "liberate women of Islam" can risk replicating the kind of colonialist and militaristic feminism condemned by many Third World feminists.

In interfaith dialogue involving Muslim women, the veil is a recurrent concern, a subject that is often politically and emotionally charged. The meaning of the veil is not monolithic and has changed over time, especially in the twentieth century. During the colonial time, the veil had come to signify the subordination of women in Muslim culture, which was seen as symptomatic of the inferiority of Islamic civilization. In the early twentieth century, Arab champions for the liberation of women, such as Qasim Amin in Egypt and Kamal Ataturk in Turkey, chastised the veil as a symbol of Muslim backwardness and encouraged women to unveil and catch up with modernity. These modern reformers argued that unless Muslim societies were modernized and Westernized, they could hardly stand up against the West's global dominance, especially its technological advance. In much of the Arab world, with the exception of women in the Arabian Peninsula, women began the process of unveiling in the first half of the twentieth century. It was not until the return of the Muslim Brotherhood to power in Egypt and the Islamic Resurgence in the 1970s that the *hijab* (headscarf) enjoyed a comeback. For the Muslim Brotherhood and Islamic groups, the veil is a fundamental Islam requirement, and a signal of the resistance of Westernization and colonialism.[43]

Across the Arab world, in Europe, and in America, there has been a resurgence of women wearing the veil since the 1970s, leading Harvard professor Leila Ahmed to call it a "silent revolution."[44] Whether to allow Muslim girls to wear the *hijab* to school has created controversies in both France and the Netherlands. In 1989, the expulsion of two French Muslim girls for wearing the *hijab* to school sparked a debate on religious freedom in France and the integration of Muslims into European societies. The influx of Muslim immigrants and asylum seekers made the Muslim population a significant minority in Europe. In 2007, the number of Muslims in the Europe was 16 million, about 3.2 percent of the population. European governments do not want to treat Islam and Muslims with exception and allow their religious organizations to exist. Yet the integration of an "ethnic minority" or a "foreign worker" population has proved to be tortuous and contentious. The French government argued that wearing the *hijab* presented obstacles to Muslim assimilation and threatened the secular principles of French nationalism. In order not to single out the Muslims, the government issued a general ban on flaunting religious symbols in public spaces.[45] In April of 2011, France became the first European country to ban face-hiding Islamic *burqas* and *niqabs*, a full-face veil with an opening for the eyes. In the Netherlands, public schools cannot ban headscarves, but can ban veils because they could impair communication. Religiously affiliated schools as special schools can enforce their own rules, and some want to ban headscarves. The debates in France and the Netherlands point to the larger issues of the construction of national culture, the rights of minorities, the norms of civil society, and the roles of government in arbitrating religious practices.

It would be a mistake to see the veil only as a religious matter, because its meaning is enmeshed in larger social, cultural, and political configurations of power. The research of Leila Ahmed has shown that the veil, which traditionally has been seen as an emblem of patriarchy and oppression of women, has been reappropriated by American Muslim women for their own empowerment. For these women, wearing the veil might mean an "affirmation of identity and community, of pride in heritage, of rejection or resistance to, or even of protest against, mainstream society."[46] After September 11, more and more American Muslim women began wearing the veil to protest against perceived discrimination and prejudice and the association of Muslims with terrorists. They want to show that Muslims exist in America and that they are not terrorists but productive members of society. Wearing the veil becomes a means of public display of identity and solidarity against Islamophobia and the general acceptance of diatribe against Islam and Muslims.

In her interviews, Leila Ahmed found that the reasons American women wear the veil might be highly personal, yet they are generically similar, often invoking a protest of injustice and a signaling of differences from the majority of society. Some of the women say that the veil is a call for justice, recalling that the veil was an anticolonial symbol in an earlier time. Instead of subordination, the veil can even be a call for gender justice, because it contests the sexism of the rules of dress in the dominant society. Others wear the veil to publicly affirm that the rights and equality of minorities need to be protected in society.[47]

Yvonne Yazbeck Haddad, who has studied American Muslim communities for more than twenty years, notes that an increasing number of adolescents and young Muslims adults are wearing the *hijab* to reclaim their identity.[48] This is contrary to the general expectation that the children of immigrants would shed their parents' religious and cultural markings to be Americanized and assimilated into the mainstream society. Since September 11, the process of re-Islamization has accelerated among some of the young American-born Muslim women. For them, the *hijab* has become a symbol of authenticity and pride. Wearing the *hijab* defies the Western demonization of Islam and the stereotypical portrayal of its extremism and debasement of women. It also shows that these women have trust in the American system that guarantees freedom of speech and religion. That these second-generation Muslim women wear the *hijab*, while their mothers' generation does not, also shows that these young women are constructing an American Islamic identity.

Women in interfaith dialogue must pay attention to the various ways Muslim women are reconstructing the meaning of the veil in the post–September 11 era, and not have a knee-jerk reaction that it invariably means submission to Islam's patriarchal teaching. At the same time, they must be more knowledgeable of Muslim women's feminist scholarship and activism. In the Christian circle, Elisabeth Schüssler Fiorenza and Phyllis Trible have pioneered the feminist interpretation of the Bible, showing that it can be read against the grain for the liberation of women. In Islam, Amina Wadud published *Qur'an and Woman* in 1992, in which she contests traditional and patriarchal interpretation of specific texts and key words that have been used to limit women's freedom and even justify violence against women.[49] Wadud points out that the original meaning of the text supports women's equality and provides a foundation to contest the discrimination of women in Muslim societies. In 2007, Laleh Bakhtiar produced *The Sublime Quran*, the first English translation by a Muslim American woman.[50] She decided to include the women's viewpoint, which has been missing in the study of the Quran. She insists that the intention of the Quran is that women and men should be complementary and not one dominating the other.

Just like feminist leaders of other faith traditions, Muslim women have exercised their agency and demanded changes in their religious institutions and communities. In 2004, Wadud and a group of women marched on the mosque at Morgantown, West Virginia, and created a new organization, the Daughters of Hajar, to reclaim Muslim women's rights. The subversive activism of these women received widespread media attention, because the cultural climate was strongly critical of conservative Islam. Then in 2005, Wadud went one step further to stage a mixed-gender congregational prayer to be led by Wadud herself. This act challenged the rule requiring the segregation of sexes during prayers, and at the same time contested the practice that women should not lead mixed-gender prayers. Seizing the moment, other progressive Muslim women worked to establish groups such as Muslim Wake-Up! and to revitalize al-Fatiha, a gay, lesbian, bisexual, and transgender Muslim organization.[51]

Jane Smith, who has participated in Christian-Muslim dialogue for many years, says that knowledge about the complex and multifaceted development of Muslim communities and women's activities would make the dialogue table feel more welcoming and open. She cautions that Muslim women sometimes express uneasiness when they feel that Christian women are pushing their "liberal" agenda onto them. In discussing women's roles in relation to men and sexual preference, some may feel uncomfortable and think that they are not appropriate topics for interfaith dialogue. Therefore, clear expectations and guidelines must be established in the beginning. In some cases, Muslim women are not comfortable participating in dialogue that involves both sexes. In traditional cultures, Muslim women do not interact with men outside their families, let alone men of other faiths. With the presence of male authority figures, Muslim women may not feel open to express their opinions or to challenge these figures. Trust and relationship must be built so that men and women become more comfortable with each other's public presence.[52]

In addition to conversation about communal concerns and social and political causes, a recent direction in Christian-Muslim dialogue has been the discussion of textual interpretation of scripture and theological issues, since there are more and more women qualified to engage in such a dialogue. Female scholars of the Hebrew Bible, New Testament, and the Quran have been brought together to discuss the authority of scripture and the ways in which they have interpreted problematic texts that demean women. An important publication is the volume *Hagar, Sarah, and Their Children*, in which noted Jewish, Christian, and Muslim scholars focus on Hagar, Sarah, and their children, from Ishmael and Isaac to their many descendants through the centuries.[53] Moving from ancient and medieval sources to contemporary interpretations and appropriations, these scholars provide an insightful review of a story that is foundational to the three traditions as an entrée for interfaith conversations. The slave girl Hagar was from Egypt, and the book includes a chapter from an African American perspective. In the Christian churches, Sarah's status is often held higher than Hagar's; in Islam, there is no distinction between the status of Hagar and Sarah and Ishmael and Isaac. The book provides many interesting angles and vantage points to look at race, class, gender, religion, and marginalized persons from this common story in three traditions.

Reciprocity and Appropriation

As women of faiths meet and dialogue with one another, the issues of reciprocity and appropriation arise because of power differentials. Judith Plaskow, a pioneer in Jewish feminist theology, recounts the following story that provides food for thought. Some time ago she participated in a heated debate about whether a U.S. Hindologist had the right to criticize some aspects of treatment of women in Hinduism. Plaskow has studied Christian theology and has criticized Paul Tillich and Reinhold Niebuhr's doctrines of sin and grace. No one has faulted Plaskow for doing so, and in fact her work has been praised and cited by Christian feminists. Plaskow notes that the U.S. Hindologist and she receive totally different treatments because they stand in different power relationships to the tradition they were studying. Christianity is the dominant tradition in the United States. Plaskow's critique of Christian theology would not be conceived as a threat, but might even be praised for contributing to a different and more nuanced understanding of the tradition.[54] The same is not true for the U.S. white feminist who studies Hinduism. There is always the danger of Orientalism to begin with. In addition, the question of insider versus outsider perspective is a tricky one if she is not a Hindu herself. Who speaks for Hinduism has become a thorny issue, since most of the people who teach and write about Hinduism in the U.S. are not Hindus themselves.

Toinette M. Eugene, an African American ethicist, notes that when women of different races, classes, religions, and sexualities gather for dialogue, existing power inequities among groups must be addressed before an alternative paradigm that values mutuality can be found. She writes, "Particularity and not universality is the condition of being heard and of expressing reciprocity and mutuality in womanist/mujerista/feminist work."[55] Because of sanctioned ignorance in our educational process and learning, the diverse groups are not equal in entering dialogue, as the dominant group is not required to know the subjugated knowledges of marginalized groups. Therefore, Eugene argues that decentering of the dominant group is essential for genuine exchange to occur, such that a variety of frameworks and a variety of ways of understanding of the world can be entertained, without constantly being forced to compare to the norm of the majority or the dominant.

In antiracist work, it is important for white people to get to know the history and struggles of people of color and not depend upon the latter to educate them. Likewise, in interfaith dialogue, participants who belong to the dominant tradition need to educate themselves on other religious traditions to level the playing field. In the U.S., more than 70 percent of adults identify themselves as Christian, and we hear far more references to the Bible in public discourse than to the Quran or the Veda. Because of the separation of church and state, students do not receive education about religious traditions in public schools. Polls have repeatedly shown that American people's religious literacy is pretty low. It is imperative to know more about other religious traditions, including the experience of both women and men, before entering into interfaith dialogue.

For Ada María Isasi-Díaz, a mujerista ethicist, respect and engagement are crucial in dialogue with others who are different from ourselves. We must respect another woman on her own terms and allow her to be herself, without demanding that she act or present herself in a way that is intelligible or acceptable to us. She writes:

> We need to enter into each other's world view as much as we can and help others open up to new perspectives. Unless we are willing to do this, the self we present to people who are different from us is a "pretend self." We will hide our real selves in order to protect ourselves from others' projections of us.[56]

Only when we are prepared to engage others with honesty, Isasi-Díaz says, can we offer another person a faithful mirror to look at her tradition, and allow other's work to challenge and stretch us, without reducing it to our view of it.

Critical and honest engagement in dialogue often means that we will not be the same after the encounter, after we have learned and gained helpful insights from others. The question of how to borrow and appropriate other women's perspectives and work has been a sensitive one among female scholars of religion. The issue goes beyond proper credit and acknowledgment of others' work, to the motivation and intention of using others to bolster our own. Feminist ethicist Mary Hunt has cautioned that it has become customary for middle-class white feminists to cite or use women of color's work in order to show that one is politically correct or cosmopolitan. An example is the endless repetition of Alice Walker's work, as if just quoting Alice Walker will make white women look less racist. She names this intellectual crime, and says, "Such crimes are often done to give the appearance of diversity all the while maintaining the model, dynamic and framework that belong to the dominant culture into which have been shoved ideas and images that do not emerge from it."[57] The mere inclusion of a few token voices without fundamentally reconsidering the operating assumptions and epistemological framework is not true diversity. Hunt urges scholars to pay attention to the ethics of borrowing, asking such questions as why we need to borrow and how to act with reciprocity with one another.

This intellectual vigilance and honesty applies not only to interaction with women of different races and faith traditions, but also to exchange within one's group. For among Jewish women, Muslim women, or Hindu women, there is a plurality of voices and differences of power. Jewish scholar Ellen M. Umansky says we need to ask, "What factors constitute sufficient similarity or commonality in deciding whose work can be appropriated?"[58] This does not mean that women scholars should feel hesitant to learn and quote from others at all, but it does mean that we acknowledge that both differences and connections exist in feminist work. Without such recognition, misuse and misappropriation of others' ideas and work will most likely occur.

Anti-Judaism and misappropriation are primary problems in Jewish-Christian dialogue and relations. Anti-Judaism has had a long history in Western history and Christian discourse. The Hebrew Scriptures have been appropriated as the Old Testament and interpreted without reference to its meaning in the Jewish tradition and rabbinic literature. The New Testament is seen as superseding the Old, since Jesus is the fulfillment of all the prophecy of the Old Testament. The new covenant brought by Jesus replaces and supersedes the old covenant between God and the Hebrew people. In parts of the New Testament, as Lawrence M. Wills has demonstrated, the Jews had been constructed as the Other and cast in negative light. This is especially so in the Gospel of John, in which the Jews are portrayed as not the true children of Abraham but the children of the devil (John 8:31–47).[59] Throughout Christian history, the Jews have been blamed for committing evil acts and a long trail of crimes, the most serious one being the killing of Jesus. Moreover, Judaism is seen as legalistic, governed by laws, whereas Christianity stresses faith, love, and life in the spirit. Judaism is criticized as ethnocentric and particular, while Christianity is seen as universal, inclusive, and open to all.

Judith Plaskow points out that to this long list of anti-Jewish motifs and themes, feminist interpreters of the New Testament have added "Jesus was a feminist," using Judaism as the negative foil.[60] The proponents of this view cite as evidence that no sexist saying is attributed to Jesus, while women were present among his followers. Jesus taught women, healed them, praised their faith, and used women's experience in some of his parables. But Plaskow argues that Jesus was not a feminist in the contemporary sense of the word, for "he is never portrayed as arguing for women's prerogatives, demanding changes in particular restrictive laws that affect women, or debating Pharisees on the subject of gender."

In order to show that Jesus was a feminist who stood out against his background, the interpreters paint a very negative picture of the treatment of women in Judaism in Jesus' time. While Jewish men did not speak to women in public, Jesus spoke to the Samaritan woman at the well. Jesus healed the woman with a twelve-year flow of blood, while she would have been considered ritually unclean in Jewish law. Jesus praised Mary for listening to his teaching, while Martha was too busy doing the women's work. Some said that Jesus was against his Jewish culture, since women were forbidden to learn the Torah. But scholars have pointed out that Jewish views about women in Jesus' period were not monolithic, and Christian feminists have selectively chosen resources and materials to support their negative contrast. Rather than seeing Jesus' attitudes toward women as part of the spectrum of Jewish attitudes and practices, these Christian feminists claim that Jesus acted against his background and was a revolutionary.

Since anti-Semitism has led to the Holocaust and other atrocities, Christian feminists must be aware of its myriad existence in Christian culture, thought, and practices. Plaskow says that Christian feminists must recognize and problematize anti-Judaism in Christian sources and traditions as a part of their feminist analyses, and discuss this issue in public. They must appreciate that Judaism is a diverse and changing tradition and not treat it as an antithesis of Christianity. In evaluating the attitude of the Jesus movement toward women, they have to take care to bring in feminist approaches to first-century Judaism. It is important to realize that rabbinic literature is not an accurate description of women's actual roles and behaviors in the first century, just as Paul's prescription about women keeping silence may not reflect women's reality at the time.[61] In fact, inscriptions have shown that Jewish women would play liturgical and leadership roles in Jewish diaspora synagogues in Jesus' time. Plaskow also specifically addresses difficulties in Jewish-Christian dialogue. She writes, "While feminists often celebrate the ways in which women's criticism and reconstruction of religion have opened up new areas of interreligious dialogue, the reality is that much Christian feminist work takes place in isolation from the Jewish feminist agenda."[62] Christian feminists often do not know or include Jewish feminists working on similar issues, and when they invite Jewish feminists to participate in dialogue, the rules of engagement are defined on Christian terms. In order to be self-critical of Christian hegemony, an appreciation of the commonalities and differences of Jewish feminist agenda is an important step.

Another tradition that has often been misappropriated is the Native American tradition, which has become very popular in the contemporary New Age movement. One can easily find workshops and seminars offering Native rituals and ceremonies to non-Native people. Many European American women are interested in Native spirituality, seeing it as earth-based and providing healing to ease the ills of modern living. Many feminists take advantage of this spiritual quest by selling sweat lodges or sacred pipe ceremonies for a profit. For Andrea Smith, a Cherokee scholar and activist, this new craze does not show respect for Native spirituality, but just the opposite. She writes, "...the New Age movement is part of a very old story of white racism and genocide against the Indian people."[63] In the colonial days, the colonizers saw that Native rituals and ceremonies held the community together, and they made them illegal. Sundances were prohibited and Indian participation in the Ghost Dance led to the Wounded Knee massacre. Today, the misappropriation of Indian spirituality continues the same genocidal practices of their ancestors. The Indian rituals are taken out of context and repackaged for white consumption and profit, without respecting their integrity and usage in Indian communities.

Smith chastises that the "Indian ways" that the New Age, white feminists practice have little grounding in reality. Indian religions are not interested in proselytizing, as in evangelical Christianity.

The spiritual leaders do not teach for a profit but feel that it is their responsibility to pass their knowledge to the future generation. In contrast with the consumerist and individualistic New Age movement, Native rituals and ceremonies are community based and reflect the needs of the community. White feminists change the context and structure of the rituals to suit their purposes and agenda, and distort the meaning of being spiritual and "Indian." They misappropriate Native cultures and religions for their own private spiritual growth and pursuit, while showing no or little accountability to the Native peoples.

Myke Johnson, a white woman who has Innu heritage, says that white people's fascination with Native spirituality has something to do with their fantasy about the Indians. There are two main stereotypes about the Indians: the "hostile savage," the dangerous warrior who attacked the settlers of the West, and the "noble savage," who was primitive, childlike, and naturally spiritual. They were those who helped and taught the Pilgrims to survive in Thanksgiving tales. What is called Native American spirituality draws on the "noble savage" stereotype, and mixes with various symbols and rituals of Native American religious practices. As the American mainstream culture becomes more secular, white people go to the margins of society to satisfy their spiritual hunger. They might be looking for an "emphasis on female deities and positive roles for women, or a focus on the earth, grounded in the interconnectedness of all beings."[64]

Johnson identifies three traps that white people might easily fall into in their reckoning with Native American people. The first is denial, which creates the myth that Indians do not exist anymore and that they are a dying race whose culture belongs to the past. This justifies taking or appropriating artifacts and elements of Native cultures in order to preserve and protect them. Another trap is the "wanting to be Indian" syndrome. White people romanticize Native culture, projecting onto it their ideals and utopia. In becoming an "Indian" they are no longer responsible for white racism. The third trap is "guilt seeking redemption." In this case, white people are aware of what has been done by white culture, but remain stuck in their guilt. They seek out Native people to forgive them and to welcome them, saying that they are okay.[65] Movies such as *Dances with Wolves* and *Avatar* are examples of this trap, showing that the white hero has turned around and been adopted by the Natives.

Andrea Smith finds that it is ironical and insulting that the misappropriation of Native religions is done in the name of feminism. She takes issue with the practice of asking a Native woman to begin a conference or a meeting with a ceremony, while there is an absence of Native participants and no attention is being paid to the pressing issues in Native communities. Under the pretense of multiculturalism, Native rituals and practices are simply coopted to service the mainstream. It is an insidious form of racism when Native people and their spirituality are not respected as a tradition with its own integrity. This does not mean that there can be no cross-cultural learning and sharing. Smith says white women who want to know the Indian ways should be involved in their political struggles and build an ongoing relationship with Native communities. Only then can true reciprocity occur and Indian people may invite them to participate in their ceremonies, on Indian terms.[66]

Multiple Identities and Hybridity

The above discussion of Orientalism, reciprocity, and appropriation brings to the fore the risks and dangers in negotiating gender and religious difference in the encounter with religious others. In Orientalism, one regards the other as stranger, as alien, as someone who is fundamentally different from oneself. In misappropriation of the other's tradition, as in the case of "wanting to be Indian," one collapses the difference, overidentifies with the other, or even reduces the other into the same. As long as we continue to use sameness and difference as the litmus test in judging persons or groups, we will continue to be trapped in the rigid categories we have created. Christian theologian Jeannine Hill Fletcher argues that we must go beyond this impasse of sameness and difference, for neither total sameness nor radical difference works in real encounters with people of other faiths. In order to go beyond the impassse, we would need to construct a new concept of identity that will allow us to theorize multiplicity and hybridity.[67]

In the past several decades, feminist theory has challenged the masculinist notion of the self as autonomous, individuated, and differentiated from others. The works of Jean Baker Miller, Nancy Chodorow, and Carol Gilligan have presented new theories about women's psychological development and moral judgment. Jean Baker Miller and her colleagues at the Stone Center at Wellesley College have put forward the "self-in-relation theory," based on women's empathy, care, and relationality with others. The self-in-relation values connection and abhors isolation, disconnection, and the loss of the other, for this would mean a fundamental loss of the self. The emphasis on relationality is important not only for women, but for human development as a whole.[68] For Fletcher, discussion of the self and human development in feminist theory offers helpful resources for constructing a more dynamic, fluid identity, one that is constantly in relation with others. Such a new concept of identity will overcome the impasse of sameness and difference by providing "a framework of interreligious encounters that allow for conversation across difference without erasing particularity and distinctiveness" (81).

Fletcher says that the use of the categories "Hindu," "Christian," "Jewish," "Buddhist," "Muslim," or "Native" as identifiable collectives defined by some common characteristics is problematic. Such a construction is based on what feminist theorist Iris Marion Young has called a "logic of identity." According to this logic, a group is bounded as a closed totality, with its borders firmly drawn, such that there is a clear distinction between insider and outsider. Fletcher points out there are two problems with using this logic to create religious identity. First, it erases the vast amount of internal diversity within a particular group by focusing on certain elements of commonalities while overlooking or suppressing difference. Second, since the collective identity is closely bound, it sharpens the distinction to those outsiders. Thus, "the logic of identity forges intra-religious solidarity through the very process of distancing otherness," Fletcher notes (85).

Labeling someone as "Christian," "Buddhist," or "Hindu" means we single out one identity—in this case religious identity—while excluding all other identities from the discourse. By so doing, someone's "Christian" identity is carved out from her other identities as mother, wife, professional, and member of a health club. No one is simply a member of a particular religion, but is also differentiated according to race, gender, class, educational level, and social and geographical locations. Each of us has multiple identities, and they cannot be easily separated from one another or compartmentalized. Fletcher says, "...each self is not the solid entity of a single identity, but rather is forged at the intersection of multiplicity of fundamentally defining features" (88). The different identities are so "entangled and interlaced" that there is no pure religious identity that is not affected by other dimensions of who we are. At times, our multiple identities might even be at odds with one another. For example, as a Catholic feminist, one might support a woman's freedom to choose, even though the Catholic magisterium upholds the sanctity of life from conception.

Fletcher argues that we are all hybrids, because we are the product of the intersection of the different categories of our identities. The category of "Hindu" or "Muslim" is not homogeneous, because the hybrid identity of each member creates internal diversity and differentiation. For Fletcher, such an understanding of hybrid identity, which challenges dualism and binarism, will help us overcome the impasse of sameness and difference in interfaith dialogue and theologies of religions. First, our hybrid identity can foster connections with members outside our group. This is because a strand of our identities has been formed relationally through interaction with other communities (90). For example, in civic engagement and in parent-teacher associations, Muslims, Hindus, and Christians relate to others as citizens and as parents or teachers. Second, hybrid identity allows for partial identification of overlapping identities, which enables collaboration across the boundaries of religious differences to occur (91). For example, feminist scholars of different traditions have collaborated on common projects and addressed common concerns, because each is simultaneously a member of a religious tradition and a feminist. In grassroots movements, women of different faiths have come together to express their solidarity and work for justice. An example is Buddhist and Christian women in Taiwan working together to protect their environment. Third, hybrid identity defies purity and allows for double or multiple religious belonging (98). In the early church, Christians drew from Greek thought and formed an overlap between categories. In our modern world, people can be both Buddhist and Jewish, or Confucian and Christian. Fourth, the understanding of hybrid identity points to identity formation as a dynamic and fluid process, such that people can change over time as a result of interaction with others (95). In interfaith dialogue, sometimes there is the fear that we will lose our religious commitment if we are open to other traditions. Such fear, however, is based on a static understanding of the self. If we understand the self as a web of relations constantly interacting with others, we will be more open to transformation and change.

I appreciate Fletcher's critique of constructing "Christianity," "Hinduism," or "Islam" as bounded or static categories in much of the discussion of theology of religions, while internal differentiation in the religious grouping is overlooked or suppressed. She is also on target when she talks about the multiplicity of the self and about hybrid identities. But there are two areas I wish she would be more explicit about and explore further, as prompted by our discussion on Orientalism and misappropriation. First, while she has stated that our different identities overlap and interact, she has not gone a step further to explicate how identities are also mutually constituted and implicated. In the discussion of Orientalism, we have seen how race is genderized and gender is racialized. Religion also comes into the picture as the treatments of women in Christianity and Islam have been crudely compared and deployed to evaluate the merits of a civilization. The sexually adventurous women in the television show *Sex and the City* are touted as liberated by Western mass media across the world, while women with the veils are often being looked upon with suspicion and curiosity. Fletcher has not sufficiently addressed how gender is politicized and enmeshed in the global struggle for cultural and political dominance.

Second, the claim that we are all hybrids has the danger of collapsing into the idea that all hybrids are the same and can participate in dialogue with open minds and on equal footing. In the discussion of cultural appropriation of Native resources, we have seen that some women need to protect their religious heritage in the face of racism and cultural genocide. They need to draw clearer boundaries about their religious and spiritual tradition, not because they are reluctant to share, but because of cultural theft and commodification. Sometimes a hybrid needs to make an ethical decision of which identity to emphasize in the work for justice. For example, Myke Johnson takes care to identify herself as white, though she is connected matrilineally to the Innu people, the people indigenous to the land that is now called Quebec and Labrador. She has grown up in white American culture, with fair skin and red hair, and decides that it is most useful for her to speak as a white woman to raise issues of the feminist spiritual movement, of which she is a part.[69]

The suggestion that we are all hybrids might camouflage or make invisible power difference, as in the liberal understanding of multiculturalism and plurality. Fletcher cites the work of Homi Bhabha, a postcolonial theorist who has popularized the idea of hybridity (99). In his classic work

The Location of Culture, Bhabha discusses hybridity in the context of colonization and the forceful imposition of one culture onto another. In such a context, the breaking down of "the symmetry and duality of self/other, inside/outside" disrupts the production of power and the boundaries of authority.[70] For Bhabha, hybridity always has an ambivalent dimension, because it signifies the fragmentation of the subject in the circuits of power at the colonial moment. In Fletcher's description of hybridity, she has not identified the ways in which this concept has been introduced in postcolonial discourse and the original context of it. In citing Bhabha, she has not spelled out that hybridity is understood by Bhabha as subversive and a form of cultural resistance in its strategic disavowal of cultural and historical difference.

When the postcolonial context and the political edge of hybridity are taken away, it can easily be coopted to glorify pluralism and multiplicity in our globalized world with free movement of trade and capital. Since everyone is a hybrid, there is really not much difference between a white feminist and a Native American woman. Everyone's cultural resources and religious artifacts are up for grabs in the big spiritual buffet. There will be little difference between a white feminist sampling Native resources for her spiritual growth and her donning a Chinese *changshan* or an Indian *shalwar kameez* to go to a party. She might be even praised for her sophisticated fine taste and cosmo-politan outlook. This scenario may not be the one that Fletcher has in mind, but we must stress that even if we are all hybrids, all the hybrids are not equal. It depends on how hybridity is used and for what purposes.

3

DIALOGUE, SOLIDARITY, AND PEACEBUILDING

Religion should be a source of compassion, care, respect, and goodwill among people, yet many horrible things have been done in the name of God and religion, including racism, colonialism, cultural genocide, and other forms of discrimination. In a speech to the United Nations Commission of Human Rights in 2001, the Nobel Peace laureate Archbishop Desmond Tutu said:

Religion has fueled alienation and conflict and has exacerbated intolerance and injustice and oppression. Some of the ghastliest atrocities have happened and are happening in the name of religion. It need not be so if we can learn the obvious: that no religion can hope to have a monopoly on God, on goodness and virtue and truth.[71]

Having devoted his life to fight against apartheid, the archbishop implored us to work harder together for mutual coexistence and tolerance. He asked us to treat our adversaries as fellow human beings deserving respect for their personhood and dignity, and not to demonize and dehumanize them.

I write this chapter less than two weeks before the tenth anniversary of September 11, 2001, when the World Trade Center and the Pentagon were attacked, killing many innocent victims and leaving many wounded. Throughout the United States, mosques, churches, synagogues, and interfaith groups are planning services or events to commemorate this fateful date. In New York, President Barack Obama, Mayor Michael Bloomberg, government officials and civic leaders, and relatives of the victims will take part in a solemn event at the World Trade Center site. The families of the victims will be allowed to go inside the memorial to find the names of their loved ones, etched into the railings at the huge waterfalls built in the footprint of the World Trade Center. The names of the nearly three thousand victims, including those who died at the Pentagon, will be read aloud for the first time.

In early May, the U.S. Navy SEALS captured and shot Osama bin Laden, leader of al-Qaeda, in his private compound in Abbottabad, Pakistan. The U.S. government has finally gotten rid of its archenemy, the most wanted face of terrorism. But does the world feel safer because bin Laden was killed and his body buried at sea? I think not. Unless we are willing to deal with the root causes that have driven many young people to join al-Qaeda and other similar militant groups, the world will not be safer. Soon after his death, bin Laden's followers vowed to retaliate.

In his statements and video interviews after September 11, bin Laden justified the attack by pointing to the injustice the American government has committed. He cited as examples the dispossession of land and mistreatment of Palestinians, the presence of the American troops in Muslims' holy land in Saudi Arabia, the cruelty of continued sanctions against Iraq, and the repressive nature of U.S.-backed antidemocratic Gulf regimes. Though we should never condone the killing of innocents, we need to ask if we have addressed these concerns of the Muslim world and done enough to alleviate the suffering of the people in this region during the intervening years. The "Arab spring" has shown the world the anger and frustration of peoples living in those ruthless and irresponsible regimes.

If the loss of life at the World Trade Center reminds us of how religious extremism can lead to violence, I hope the remembrance of this horrifying incident will galvanize people of all faiths to recommit ourselves for peace.

On the day before the tenth anniversary of

September 11, a group of Muslims will hold a conference in Washington, DC, to remember the victims and to explore mercy and compassion as the core messages in the Islamic heritage. Speakers will include members of the three Abrahamic faiths. American Muslim leaders remind us that among the three thousand who died, about sixty were Muslims. Imam Zaik Shakir, chair of the organization United for Change, which is planning the conference, says, "We will not allow the distortion of our religious teachings, and the baseless caricaturing of our community to lead us to respond to the challenges of our day in a merciless fashion."[72]

The National Council of Churches in the United States has provided worship resources for member churches for commemorating September 11. The General Secretary Michael Kinnamon said in a statement, "For Christians in the U.S. and around the world, this will be a time of prayer and remembrance of those who were lost, as well as a time for each of us to seek to discern God's will for ending the hatred and resentments that spawned the violence."[73] The "Litany of Remembrance, Penitence, and Hope" laments that Americans have sought revenge out of fear and shock, and acknowledges that peace will come only when the concerns of justice become the subject of political and social goodwill everywhere.[74]

Peacebuilding should be a primary focus of

interfaith dialogue in the future. In the past several years, a group of theologians has begun to explore the concept of polydoxy in order to describe the multiplicity and relationality of God and of our world. Polydoxy, as its prefix "poly" suggests, acknowledges both the internal diversity of the Christian tradition and the plurality of the world's religious and spiritual traditions. Colleen Hartung has said, "Polydoxy, a space for many opinions about belief within a body of belief, or alternatively a place of many faiths within a circle of faith, implies an openness to diversity, difference, challenge, and multiplicity."[75] This chapter explores the rich meanings of polydoxy and discusses its implications for interreligious solidarity and concrete actions for peacebuilding.

Polydoxy and Divine Multiplicity

Believing that one's religion is the ultimate truth and infinitely superior to others can easily lead to intolerance, prejudice, and exclusivity. When this kind of belief is combined with racial and ethnic bigotry, perceived discrimination and injustice, and the hope for political revenge, violence and even holy war may occur. When Mohammed Atta and other members of the al-Qaeda network boarded the planes that plunged into the World Trade Center, they thought they were carrying out Allah's will to punish Americans because of their great crimes. The Norwegian Anders Behring Breivik is a right-wing fundamentalist Christian who preaches hatred in his blogs, accusing Islam of killing 300 million people and Muslims of trying to take over Oslo and other European cities. Religious conflicts exist not only between Muslims and Christians, because when we look at the world at large, we can see that violence has also been committed by believers of other religious traditions, such as Sikhs and Hindus in India, Buddhists and Hindus in Sri Lanka, and Jews and Muslims in Palestine.

As we have seen, theologians have offered various ways to address religious plurality and diversity in a nonexclusive way, from Karl Rahner's "anonymous Christian," John Hick's "God has many names," and Mark Heim's "different salvations," to Jeannine Hill Fletcher's "we are all hybrids." Each of these theologians affirmed that we have much to learn from other faith traditions and that Christianity does not have an exclusive claim to truth. A group of scholars working in constructive theology has suggested the term *polydoxy* to capture the idea that Christians do not have a monopoly on God's revelation and that divinity should be understood in terms of multiplicity, open-endedness, and relationality.

The theoretically rich concept of polydoxy draws from multiple sources, including feminist, pluralist, poststructuralist, and process theories.[76]

Feminist and poststructuralist thinkers such as Luce Irigaray, Jacques Derrida, and Gilles Deleuze have long debunked the tyranny of the "one"—be it the phallus, the father's law, monotheism, or logocentrism. Process philosophy describes the world not in static terms, but as open-ended processes and ever-becoming, allowing quarks, chaos, and creativity to occur. Polydoxy is influenced by critical social theory, which eschews top-down authority and advocates radical democracy and grassroots participation. It celebrates globalization from below and the "network thinking" of what Michael Hardt and Antonio Negri described as the emergent "multitude."[77] Finally, polydoxy is also informed by contemporary trinitarian thought, which stresses mutuality and relation of the Triune God. The early church fathers' concept of *perichoresis*—the interpenetration and indwelling of the Father, Son, and Holy Spirit—has been reinvigorated in the development of a social ontology.

Polydoxy highlights the plurality within the Christian tradition and the historically contingent nature of the formulation of so-called orthodoxy. Christians have four Gospels, which cannot be collapsed into a single account. The diversity of the Hebrew Bible and the other early works that have been excluded from the canon testify to the multiple and complex sources of Christianity. Throughout Christian history, multiple theological traditions and different theological schools existed

71

alongside one another, resulting in vigorous debates and dissent. Even though the early ecumenical councils produced creeds and formulated doctrines, the whole church did not accept and abide by them. For instance, after the Nestorians were condemned as heretical by the church councils because of their understanding of Christology, they continued to preach, and established churches in India and China. Polydoxy insists that no theology or creed can exhaust the meaning of God and claim doctrinal finality. It underscores the limitations of human language and the contingency of human thought. Polydoxy shares affinity with apophatic theology, which insists that the nature of God cannot be fully described, and we can only talk about what God is not, rather than what God is.

Polydoxy requires us to debunk and demystify the logic of the One, and especially of monotheism. Laurel C. Schneider points out that the term *monotheism* does not appear until 1680, and the concept has been used by white European and American social scientists to classify religions either as monotheistic or polytheistic and to justify the ideology of European cultural and religious superiority. She writes:

> "Monotheism," as a designation of progressive advancement, is attached to the Jewish-to-Christian trajectory of western European history, a trajectory that purportedly begins

in prehistoric polytheism, advances to pre-liminary monotheism in Israel, and finally reaches full flower and sophistication in Christianity, all through the revelatory acts of God.[78]

Instead of monotheism and the logic of the One, Schneider proposes a theology of divine multiplicity, which recognizes the limitations of all our metaphors for God, such as Father, Logos, Ground of Being, King of Kings, and Lord of Lords. The logic of multiplicity that she introduces is fundamentally fluid, fluent, or supple.[79] Divine multiplicity is characterized by fluidity because it is ever changing, without closures and endings. Learning to become fluent in our speaking of God implies "a willingness to enter into a flow of language that is ever shifting, diving into language without much of a net, without mechanical or predictable outcomes."[80] Suppleness implies a willingness to delve into the gray area and to refuse to resolve questions about the is-ness and isn't-ness of God in any absolute sense. Since the logic of multiplicity denies the ontological status of eternity and stasis, it undermines any permanent and absolute claims of religion, patriotism, and identities, which have justified wars, conflicts, and violence.

Polydoxy does not use terms such as *omnipotent, unchanging, the unmovable mover,* or *the First Cause* to describe God's relation with creation. Just as the divine is forever becoming, creation is never static, following a fixed trajectory from the beginning to the end. Creation is not once for all, but a continuous, unfolding process, with creativity, novelty, and chance. Polydoxy supports the critique of ecofeminist theologians, who challenge a dualistic, hierarchical, and androcentric doctrine of creation that puts human beings, and especially men, at the center of the universe. Such a doctrine justifies the subordination of women and nonhuman species, and the erroneous thought that nature has utilitarian value and exists for the benefits of humans. For Brazilian ecofeminist theologian Ivone Gebara, *trinity* refers not only to the Godhead, but is a symbolic expression of the interrelatedness, communion, and reciprocity of all life in a continuous and dynamic process of creativity. In the cosmos, trinity manifests as multiplicity and interdependence of the stars and galaxies. On earth, trinity is shown in the interconnectedness of all life forms and the movement toward cosmic citizenship, beyond the confines of national boundaries and particular locale.[81]

Polydoxy foregrounds the diversity of cultural and religious traditions of the world, and sees such diversity as a blessing and not a curse. Theologian John Thatamanil says that religious diversity is a natural outcome and expression of human encounter with divine multiplicity. He notes that many trinitarian theologies of religious pluralism have first developed their concept of trinity in Christian terms and then entered into dialogue with people of other faiths. He asks, "Might it be possible for Christian theologians to envision a trinitarian engagement with religious diversity that is marked by a sense of *anticipation* that other traditions may have something to teach us about how to think even about trinity?"[82] He invites us to imagine trinity as an open site for interreligious dialogue and proceeds to show how the Christian trinitarian understanding can be enriched by the Hindu and Buddhist traditions. He refers to God as ground, contingency, and relation by bringing Hindu, Christian, and Buddhist ideas into creative dialogue. From the writings of Śankara and the Upanishads, the ultimate (Brahman) is immanent as ground and transcendent as mystery. From the Jewish and Christian tradition, the worth and singular value of each and every element in creation is affirmed. The human predicament is seen in terms of contingency, affirming the particularity of embodied selves and the concreteness of human encounters and relationships. From the Buddhist tradition, the notion of emptiness points out that nothing exists by itself and has its own-being. Nothing exists outside of relation, and egoism represents a false consciousness that the self can exist in isolation from others. Such a trinitarian vision respects the differences between and within religious traditions and enables us to move deeper into dialogue and communion with non-Christian neighbors. Thatamanil writes, "Inasmuch as polydoxy is a vision of many-in-relation (multiplicity), a many that does not negate the one, this speculative trinitarianism is most assuredly polydoxic."[83]

Thatamanil has worked in the field of comparative theology for many years. Comparative theology is a relatively new field, and scholars working in this field need to study carefully a tradition that is not their own. The sources of comparative theology are drawn from multiple religious and theological traditions, and its method of procedure is shaped by a comparative study of the sources at hand. As a Christian theologian and an ordained priest, Thatamanil is drawn to Buddhism and says that we need to develop a binocular religious vision for our age.[84] He explains that Buddhism appeals to him, not because there is something deficient in his own tradition, but "to deepen [his] experience of the world by entering into another way of understanding and being." He calls it a binocular religious vision, because it has "the capacity to see the world through more than one set of religious lenses and to integrate into one life, insofar as possible, what is disclosed through those lenses." He cites as example Gandhi, whose "theory and practice of nonviolent resistance integrated ideas and practices drawn from Jainism, Christianity (Jesus' Sermon on the Mount in particular), and, of course, Hinduism." His trinitarian formulation of

God as ground, contingency, and relation is an example of his binocular religious vision at work.

Interreligious Solidarity

Polydoxy debunks the myth of the superiority of one God, one creed, and one church, and holds multiple traditions and perspectives together when looking at God and reality. A theology of multiplicity seeks company and does not reduce the Other into the Same. Marion Grau says that polydoxy contains a measure of the paradoxical, because it holds multiple contingencies in tension. "It resists claims to strict *orthodoxy*, if by that we mean the lifting up of one particular opinion as true. But it is in, and about, orthodoxy as a discourse interested in reliable, resolute, and responsible claims to validity."[85] Polydoxy goes beyond the liberal claims that all religions are equally valid, for it asserts that we cannot know our own tradition without seeing it in relation to and through the lens offered by other religious and spiritual traditions.

Polydoxy opens more room for dialogue since it releases the pressure of having to defend one's singular identity, because the boundaries of the self and of one's tradition are constantly shifting. Interreligious solidarity is both possible and necessary because we do not exist in our cultural, linguistic, and religious enclaves, isolated from one another. Globalization and postmodernity have brought us much closer to each other and what happens to one religious community affects the prospects and livelihood of other communities. We are not defined by the communal and social practices of our religious community alone, because we simultaneously belong to and participate in many overlapping communities.

In order for the Christian churches to express interreligious solidarity with people of other faiths, churches must own up to their collusion with the long history of colonialism and cultural imperialism. In *Empire and the Christian Tradition*, contributors have surveyed the intricate relationship between theology and empire from Paul to modern times.[86] Since its beginning, Christian theology has borrowed the language, idioms, and metaphors of the Roman Empire. As Catherine Keller has said, "When [Christianity] opened its young mouth to speak, it spoke in the many tongues of empire—nations and languages colonized by Rome, and before that Greece, and before that Babylon, which had first dispersed the Jews into imperial space."[87] Throughout the ages, Christian theologians have the complicated relation of being coopted by empire at times and having to resist empire at other times. In the modern colonial period, Christian churches colluded with colonialism through their mission of "civilizing" the natives, by superimposing Western norms and cultures on other peoples. The works of R. S. Sugirtharajah and other postcolonial critics have demonstrated how the Bible has been enlisted to support imperial claims and cultural hegemony.[88] The Great Commission to make disciples of all nations (Matt 28:19), for example, was cited during the colonial days to justify the mandate to convert other peoples and to condemn other religions as false and idolatrous.

To strengthen interreligious solidarity in our postcolonial world, theologian Hyo-Dong Lee turns to the work of Hegel on mutual recognition as a possible resource.[89] For Hegel, mutual recognition is based on free agency, devoid of domination and exclusion, so that each one's freedom is protected and maintained. In a master-slave relation, mutual recognition is not possible because the slave has no genuine freedom and is dependent on the master. Though Hegel's formulation of mutual recognition is limited to individuals within a single community, his theory can also be applicable to relations among communities and nations. In our postcolonial situation, the importance of "participatory parity" must be emphasized, because of the power differential among different groups and communities. Without leveling the playing field, recognition by the dominant party can simply be a form of "tolerance" or even a thinly veiled contempt. Franz Fanon's *Black Skin, White Masks* describes poignantly the complex dialectics of the psyche of the colonizers and the colonized. Even though the white master may be forced to recognize the black slave's free agency out of fear, he still regards the slave as inferior to himself.[90]

Formerly colonized peoples and marginalized others have been historically isolated and separated from one another because of lack of resources and the use of divide and rule tactics. The biggest challenge for interreligious solidarity in our postcolonial condition is how to enable the subalterns to mutually recognize one another and create a political solidarity narrative to galvanize support. The term *subaltern* was coined by Antonio Gramsci to refer to persons who are socially, politically, and culturally outside the hegemonic power structures. Postcolonial critics have been especially concerned about the plight of the female subalterns, who are often excluded from self-representation and are spoken for by others. Thus Lee asks, "Will it be possible for poor African Christian women and poor Asian Muslim women likewise to weave their stories together into a unifying narrative of interreligiously hybrid identity that indicts and counters the overwhelming economic, political, cultural, and religious forces arrayed against them to 'put them in their place'?"[91]

If we survey the global scene, we will see that peacebuilding has become a very powerful rallying point and unifying narrative for grassroots women of different faiths to mutually recognize one another and work in solidarity. An example is the Women in Black movement, an interfaith grassroots women's movement whose motto is "For justice, against war." The movement first started in January 1988, one month after the first Palestinian Intifada broke out, when small groups of Israeli and Palestinian women stood once a week at a major intersection in Israel/Palestine. Dressed in black, they stood in silent vigils, holding up a black sign with "Stop the Occupation" written on it. In many cultures, the color symbolizes mourning, and wearing black is a public gesture of mourning and bearing witness to the atrocities of violence. The movement quickly spread to other countries and has become "a world-wide network of women committed to peace with justice and actively against injustice, war, militarism, and other forms of violence."[92] When Women in Black called for vigils in 2001 against the occupation of Palestinian lands, at least 150 Women in Black groups from around the world responded.

Members of Women in Black come from many national, ethnic, and religious backgrounds, and together they want to educate and influence public opinion to stop war and violence. These women employ nonviolent and nonaggressive forms of actions, such as sitting down to block a road, entering forbidden zones, refusing to comply with orders, and bearing witness. During the Gulf War in 1991, a group of women in London demonstrated as Women against War in the Gulf. Later, some of the women renamed themselves Women in Black. Soon after, when the war in the former Yugoslavia broke out, Women in Black was formed in Belgrade in 1991 to oppose masculine violence and nationalist aggression. Women in Black in India has protested against religious conflicts and violence. Formed in 1992, Women in Black sprang into action when Babri Masjid, an ancient mosque, was torn down by Hindu fundamentalists and women were the main victims in the violence that engulfed India. They stood every Thursday in silent vigils on the streets in Bangalore, in the market squares, and in the Gandhi Peace Park to protest violence against women.[93]

In the post–September 11 era, women's interfaith initiatives have gained ground in many parts of the United States. These initiatives were motivated by a strong sense of community building after a crisis, formed by personal invitation from an individual to other persons or groups, and oriented toward common action in the form of group or social projects. They are different from the standard model of interfaith engagements, since they are led by women of the community and not by clergy or academics or professionals in interfaith relations. Instead of formal conversations on doctrines, these women use storytelling to share personal testimonies, reflections, and daily struggles when conflicts of identity occur. After September 11, Betsy Wiggins in Syracuse, New York, wanted to reach out to Muslim women in her community. She found Danya Wellmon, and the two invited other women to join them for dialogue and sharing. They formed the group Women Transcending Barriers, which continues to meet monthly for storytelling, service, and socializing. The group includes Muslim, Christian, Buddhist, and Jewish women. In southern Florida, an interfaith group called JAM & ALL was founded by a Jew and a Muslim. The group of Muslim, Jewish, and Christian women is dedicated to fostering understanding, social harmony, and peace through dialogue, multicultural interaction, and educational projects. Similar groups have been formed in California, Washington State, and other parts of the United States. The Pluralism Project at Harvard has convened conferences and meetings, bringing women of different faiths together to exchange views and to network.[94]

Dialogue and Peacebuilding

The tragedy of September 11, 2001, has prompted many people to reflect on the historical relation between religion and violence. More wars have been waged and more people have been killed in the name of religion than by any other institutional force in history. President George W.

Bush's use of the inflammatory terms *Crusade* and *axis of evil* was inappropriate and most unfortunate, because these terms rekindled the lengthy history of "holy war" against the infidels. Couched in apocalyptic metaphors, war and violence were justified by appealing to the ultimate confrontation between God and Satan, good and evil, and light and darkness, and by the assurance of total victory and the annihilation of the enemies. As we remember the events of September 11, we should listen to John L. Esposito, an authority on the Islamic world, who says, "It is not a time for provoking the clash of civilizations or for the self-fulfilling prophecy that such a clash is inevitable. It is rather a time for global engagement and coalition building, for the active promotion of coexistence and cooperation."[95]

Mark Juergensmeyer has studied the global rise of religious terrorism and the cultures of violence via case studies in the wide spectrum of Christianity, Judaism, Islam, Hinduism, Sikhism, and Buddhism. He shows that religious violence is "performative violence," in that the acts of violence are "performative events" aiming to make a symbolic statement. Violent acts and bloodshed become justifiable when they are imbued with ultimate religious meaning. He writes:

These acts, although terribly real, have been sanitized by becoming symbols; they have been stripped of their horror by being invested with religious meaning. They have been justified and thereby exonerated as part of a religious template that is even larger than myth and history. They are elements of a ritual scenario that makes it possible for the people involved to experience safely the drama of a cosmic war.[96]

When people suffer from economic destitution, social alienation, and political repression, Juergensmeyer notes, the religious image of cosmic struggle gives hope and meaning to such bitter experiences, and the participation in a grand conflict may even seem to be exhilarating. He says that there are three reasons why violence has accompanied religion's renewed presence in the political sphere at the present moment. The first is religion's propensity to absolutize and to project images of cosmic war. The second is the huge gap between the haves and the have-nots and social tensions that demand some kinds of redress and absolute solutions. The third is the sense of personal humiliation felt by some people, who demand that their dignity and integrity be recognized and restored in the global shifts of power. At the end of his book *Terror in the Mind of God*, Juergensmeyer concludes that religious violence will only end with some moderation of religion's passion and some acknowledgment of religion in elevating social and spiritual values of public life.[97]

Interfaith dialogue can contribute to the promotion of goodwill and mutual recognition of various religious and civic groups in public life. Instead of letting right-wing fundamentalists or religious fanatics speak for their tradition, religious leaders and people of faith can share their resources for nonviolence and peacebuilding. In the Christian tradition, Jesus has advocated for nonviolence and instructed his disciples to turn the other cheek, go the second mile, and give up the cloak. But Jesus' teaching on nonviolence has often been misunderstood. Nonviolence does not mean submission, meekness, and passivity, as shown evidently in Jesus' own life and ministry. Jesus confronted the Roman imperial authority and Jewish religious hierarchy, even died on the cross. In our modern time, the life and work of Martin Luther King, Jr., during the Civil Rights movement best exemplified what Jesus meant and taught. During the Montgomery bus boycott, the boycotters were physically attacked and King was jailed for his involvement. King taught his followers about the power of nonviolence. He said the aim of nonviolent resistance is not to humiliate or to defeat the opponent, but to win his or her friendship and understanding. Its goal is to attack the evil system that oppresses people, and not to attack individuals who are caught up in the system. He writes, "The end of violence or the aftermath of violence is bitterness. The aftermath of nonviolence is reconciliation and the creation of a beloved community."[98] Nonviolent action is based on the Christian understanding of agapic love, the overflowing love of God for all persons that is creative and redemptive. As King says:

It not only avoids external violence or external physical violence but also internal violence of spirit. And so at the center of our movement stood the philosophy of love. The attitude that the only way to ultimately change humanity and make for the society that we all long for is to keep love at the center of our lives.[99]

While King was leading the Civil Rights movement, the Vietnamese Zen master Thich Nhat Hanh advocated peace during the Vietnam War through teaching and practicing what he called Engaged Buddhism. He organized youths for social service and provided services to war victims through education, health care, and economic development in the war-torn city of Saigon. Nhat Hanh met King and the Trappist monk Thomas Merton during a speaking tour in the United States sponsored by the Fellowship of Reconciliation, a pacifist organization. When King became outspoken against the Vietnam War and American foreign policy in Southeast Asia, he nominated Nhat Hanh to receive the Nobel Peace Prize in 1967, hailing him as his friend and an apostle of peace and nonviolence.

If King drew from Christian agapic love as the base for nonviolent action, Nhat Hanh's Engaged Buddhism teaches the Buddhist ideal of compassion—cosuffering with all beings. Compassion for people we like and people we don't like is based on a profound recognition that we are infinitely connected to one another and we are not isolated. Nhat Hanh uses the term *interbeing* to describe that everything is in everything else, the one is the all and the all are the one. He writes, "To be is to inter-be. You cannot just *be* by yourself alone. You have to inter-be with every other thing."[100] One can cultivate compassion and forgiveness for one's enemy if one recognizes that one's actions are not random acts, but are shaped by personal history, life circumstances, and other people around one. Nhat Hanh invites us to put ourselves in our enemy's shoes and imagine that we are also imperfect beings capable of doing malicious or even violent acts.

Nhat Hanh has written prolifically and taught about peace and peacemaking throughout the world. In exile from Vietnam after the Communists took over, he set up Plum Village in southwest France near Bordeaux as a meditation center to teach the practice of mindfulness to visitors from all over the world. He has also toured the United States, leading retreats and teaching mindful living to Vietnam veterans, prison inmates, police officers, and members of the Congress. Just a few days after the attack on September 11, 2001, he preached nonviolence and forgiveness in a memorable speech at the Riverside Church in New York City. In *Peace Is Every Step*, Nhat Hanh speaks about peacemaking as a daily practice, to be actualized in the mundane things that we do.[101] He regards meditation as a powerful tool for peacemaking because it helps us to be in touch with our true self and become aware of the suffering as well as the hope in our world. He writes:

> Meditation is to be aware of what is going on—in our bodies, in our feelings, in our minds, in our world. Each day 40,000 children die of hunger. The superpowers now have more than 50,000 nuclear warheads, enough to destroy our planet many times. Yet the sunrise is beautiful, and the rose that bloomed this morning along the wall is a miracle. Life is both dreadful and wonderful. To practice meditation is to be aware of both aspects.[102]

His Holiness the Dalai Lama, the Nobel Prize winner of 1989, has been an ardent supporter of interfaith dialogue for peace and peacebuilding for numerous years. Based on his encounter with the world's religious leaders and his interactions with many religious communities, he has written the book *Toward a True Kinship of Faiths*.[103] He notes that religion has become a very divisive force in our present world and there is increasing polarization between the religious and those with no religion. As one of the world's eminent spiritual leaders, he sees the promotion of interreligious understanding and harmony as his life commitment. He challenges religious believers to accept the full worth of faith traditions other than their own. For him, the line between exclusivism and fundamentalism is a narrow one; the line between fundamentalism and extremism is even narrower.[104]

In perusing the world's different faiths, including the Hindu, Christian, Islamic, Jewish, and Buddhist traditions, the Dalai Lama says we do not need to accept that all religions are fundamentally the same or that they lead to the same place before we can work together in solidarity. We can discern the underlying commonalities among the different traditions in promoting genuine interreligious understanding and harmony. He affirms:

> My engagement with the world's religions has convinced me that, whatever the differences of doctrine, on the level of actually living a religious life or fulfilling a spiritual aspiration, there is a striking degree of shared

understanding. In particular, all the great religions stress compassion as a fundamental spiritual value.[105]

The Dalai Lama discusses the challenge of religion and violence in the world and the enormous role religion can play to enhance the common good. He says that it is important for every major faith tradition to acknowledge that it has served and has the potential to serve as a cause for division, hatred, and conflict. Instead of pointing our fingers at others, we need to enter into a self-educational process and be vigilant against all forms of chauvinism, bigotry, and violence. People of all faiths need to stand firm against violence and speak out against religious extremists when they hijack religious language and dogma to justify their aberrant acts. Religion serves the cause of violence when it is adopted as "an identity label that, instead of being a spiritual path to one's humanity, becomes a marker by which one defines oneself as opposed to others."[106] Using Buddhist terminology, he says that when that happens, religion can become a source of attachment and aversion, causing disharmony, harm, and division.

Yet, the Dalai Lama continues to believe that religion can be a tremendous force for good. For out of the common ground of compassion, religious institutions and communities of committed individuals can come together and act positively for the common good. He even cites the words of St. Paul: "...faith can move mountains." The power of religion, for him, lies in "its special appeal to the whole range of human psyche, including most importantly our emotions, against the backdrop of a vision of ultimate truth, with its provision of meaning and purpose."[107] The time has come, he says, to channel this valuable resource to address many problems humanity faces today, such as the protection of the environment, the inequities of poverty, and the ethical dilemmas brought by scientific knowledge and technology. We would be wise to heed the Dalai Lama's call.

NOTES

1. Claude Lefort, "The Permanence of the Theologico-Political," in *Political Theologies: Public Religion in a Post-Secular World*, ed. Hent de Vries and Lawrence E. Sullivan (New York: Fordham University Press, 2006), 148–87.

2. Samuel P. Huntington, *The Clash of Civilizations and the Remaking of World Order* (New York: Simon and Schuster, 1996).

3. Tu Weiming, "Family, Nation, and the World," Reischauer Lecture, Harvard University, April 1996. http://tuweiming.com/lecture.3.html.

4. "Introduction," in *Religions/Globalizations: Theories and Cases*, ed. Dwight N. Hopkins, Lois Ann Lorentzen, Eduardo Mendieta, and David Batstone (Durham, NC: Duke University Press, 2001), 2–3. See also Rebecca Todd Peters, *In Search of the Good Life: The Ethics of Globalization* (New York: Continuum, 2004).

5. Thomas Banchoff, "Introduction," in *Religious Pluralism, Globalization, and World Politics*, ed. Thomas Banchoff (New York: Oxford University Press, 2008), 8.

6. Ibid., 10.

7. Ibid., 11.

8. Mark Juergensmeyer, "2009 Presidential Address: Beyond Words and War: The Global Future of

Religion," *Journal of the American Academy of Religion* 78 (2010): 887.

9. Paul F. Knitter, *Introducing Theologies of Religions* (Maryknoll, NY: Orbis Books, 2002), 66.

10. Heinrich Denzinger, *Enchiridion Symbolorum, definitionum et declarationum de rebus fidei et morum*, 34th ed. (Barcione: Herder, 1967), 1351, as quoted in Francis Sullivan, *Salvation Outside the Church? Tracing the History of the Catholic Response* (New York: Paulist Press, 1992), 6.

11. Peter Beyer, *Religions in Global Society* (London: Routledge, 2006), 72–74.

12. Tomoko Masuzawa, *The Invention of Religions, or, How European Universalism Was Preserved in the Language of Pluralism* (Chicago: University of Chicago Press, 2005), xiv.

13. Diana L. Eck, *A New Religious America: How a "Christian Country" Has Become the World's Most Religiously Diverse Nation* (San Francisco: HarperSanFrancisco, 2001).

14. Diana L. Eck and the Pluralism Project at Harvard University, *On Common Ground: World Religions in America* (New York: Columbia University Press, 1997) and the Web site of the Pluralism Project, http://pluralism.org.

15. John Orr, "Los Angeles Is the Most Religiously Diverse City in the World," http://www.prolades.com/glama/CRCC%20demographics%20%20Los%20Angeles.htm.

16. Jerrilynn Dodds, "Nothing New about Mosques in New York," in *CNN Opinion* Web site, http://articles.cnn.com/2010-08-04/opinion/dodds.mosques.new.

york_1_first-mosque-new-mosque-small-mosque?_s=
PM:OPINION.

17. Diana L. Eck, "What Is Pluralism?" at the Pluralism Project Web site, http://pluralism.org/pages/pluralism/what_is_pluralism.

18. John Milbank, "The End of Dialogue," in *Christian Uniqueness Reconsidered: The Myth of a Pluralistic Theology of Religions*, ed. Gavin D'Costa (Maryknoll, NY: Orbis Books, 1990), 175.

19. Stanley Hauerwas and William H. Willimon, *Resident Aliens: A Provocative Christian Assessment of Culture and Ministry for People Who Know That Something Is Wrong* (Nashville: Abingdon, 1989), 41.

20. Stanley Hauerwas, "The End of Religious Pluralism: A Tribute to David Burrell," in *Democracy and New Religious Pluralism*, ed. Thomas Banchoff (New York: Oxford University Press, 2007), 284.

21. Raimon Panikkar, "The Jordan, the Tiber, and the Ganges," in *The Myth of Christian Uniqueness: Toward a Pluralistic Theology of Religions*, ed. John Hick and Paul F. Knitter (Maryknoll, NY: Orbis Books, 1987), 95.

22. Peter C. Phan, "Mission and Interreligious Dialogue: Edinburgh, Vatican II, and Beyond." Paper presented at the 2010 Boston Conference, November 6, 2010.

23. Diana L. Eck, *Encountering God: A Spiritual Journey from Bozeman to Banaras* (Boston: Beacon, 1993), 214.

24. "Dialogue between Men of Living Faiths: The Ajaltoun Memorandum," in *Dialogue between Men of*

Living Faiths, ed. S. J. Samartha (Geneva: World Council of Churches, 1971), 107–17.

25. The document was issued by the Pontifical Council for Interreligious Dialogue. The following summary is based on Maria Hornung, *Encountering Other Faiths* (New York: Paulist Press, 2007), 27–30.

26. These approaches are helpfully discussed in Knitter, *Introducing Theologies of Religions*.

27. John Hick, *An Interpretation of Religion: Human Responses to the Transcendent* (New Haven: Yale University Press, 1989).

28. S. Mark Heim, *Salvations: Truth and Difference in Religions* (Maryknoll, NY: Orbis Books, 1995), 149.

29. Aloysius Pieris, *An Asian Theology of Liberation* (Maryknoll, NY: Orbis Books, 1988), 87.

30. Raimon Panikkar, *The Intrareligious Dialogue* (New York: Paulist Press, 1978), 40.

31. Raimon Panikkar, *The Cosmotheandric Experience: Emerging Religious Consciousness* (Maryknoll, NY: Orbis Books, 1993).

32. Catherine Cornille, ed., *Many Mansions? Multiple Religious Belonging and Christian Identity* (Maryknoll, NY: Orbis Books, 2002).

33. Judith A. Berling, *A Pilgrim in Chinese Culture: Negotiating Religious Diversity* (Maryknoll, NY: Orbis Books, 1997), 38.

34. Mark Juergensmeyer, *Terror in the Mind of God: The Global Rise of Religious Violence*, 3rd ed. (Berkeley: University of California Press, 2003), 6–7.

35. Ibid., 15.

36. Ursula King, "Feminism: The Missing Dimension in the Dialogue of Religion," in *Pluralism and the*

Religions: The Theological and Political Dimensions (London: Cassell, 1998), 44–46.

37. Dulcie Abraham et al., eds., *Faith Renewed: A Report of the First Asian Women's Consultation on Interfaith Dialogue* (Hong Kong: Asian Women's Resource Centre for Culture and Theology, 1989), and A. Prasetya Murniati and Marlene Perera, eds., *Drink from Our Own Resources for Creative Ripples: A Feminist Theology for Hope through Inter-faith Dialogue from a Holistic Perspective* (Maggona, Sri Lanka: EATWOT Women's Commission, Asia, n.d.).

38. Rita M. Gross, *Feminism and Religion: An Introduction* (Boston: Beacon Press, 1996), 245.

39. Edward W. Said, *Orientalism* (New York: Vantage, 1979), 2.

40. Jasmin Zine, "Between Orientalism and Fundamentalism: The Politics of Muslim Women's Feminist Engagement," *Muslim World Journal of Human Rights* 3, no. 1 (2006): 4.

41. Ibid., 1.

42. Gayatri Chakravorty Spivak, "Can the Subaltern Speak?" in *Marxism and the Interpretation of Culture*, ed. Cary Nelson and Lawrence Grossberg (Urbana, IL: University of Illinois Press, 1988), 296–97.

43. Leila Ahmed, *A Quiet Revolution: The Veil's Resurgence, from the Middle East to America* (New Haven: Yale University Press, 2011), 19–92.

44. Ibid.

45. Yvonne Yazbeck Haddad and Tyler Golson, "Overhauling Islam: Representation, Construction, and Cooption of 'Moderate Islam' in Western Europe," *Journal of Church and State* 49, no. 3 (2007): 492.

46. Ahmed, *A Quiet Revolution*, 210.

47. Ibid., 211.

48. Yvonne Yazbeck Haddad, "The Post 9/11 *Hijab* as Icon," *Sociology of Religion* 68, no. 3 (2007): 253–67.

49. Amina Wadud-Muhsin, *Qu'ran and Women* (Kuala Lumpur: Penerbit Fajar Bakti Sdn. Bhd., 1992).

50. Laleh Bakhtiar, *The Sublime Quran* (Chicago: Kazi, 2007).

51. Ahmed, *A Quiet Revolution*, 272–74.

52. Jane Idleman Smith, *Muslims, Christians, and the Challenge of Interfaith Dialogue* (New York: Oxford University Press, 2007), 146–50.

53. Phyllis Trible and Letty M. Russell, eds., *Hagar, Sarah, and Their Children: Jewish, Christian, and Muslim Perspectives* (Louisville, KY: Westminster John Knox Press, 2006).

54. Judith Plaskow, "Appropriation, Reciprocity, and Issues of Power," in *Feminist Theological Ethics: A Reader*, ed. Lois K. Daly (Louisville, KY: Westminster John Knox Press, 1994), 100.

55. Toinette M. Eugene, "On 'Difference' and the Dream of Pluralist Feminism," in *Feminist Theological Ethics*, 93.

56. Ada María Isasi-Díaz, "Viva la Diferencia!" in *Feminist Theological Ethics*, 95.

57. Mary Hunt, "Commentary," in *Feminist Theological Ethics*, 106.

58. Ellen M. Umansky, "Commentary," in *Feminist Theological Ethics*, 114.

59. Lawrence M. Wills, *Not God's People: Insiders and Outsiders in the Biblical World* (Lanham, MD: Rowman and Littlefield, 2008), 150–52.

60. Judith Plaskow, "Anti-Judaism in Feminist Christian Interpretation," in *Searching the Scriptures*, vol. 1, *A Feminist Introduction*, ed. Elisabeth Schüssler Fiorenza (New York: Crossroad, 1993), 119–22.

61. Ibid., 124–26.

62. Ibid., 127.

63. Andrea ("Andy") Smith, "For All Those Who Were Indians in a Former Life," *Ms. Magazine* (November/December, 1991): 44.

64. Myke Johnson, "Wanting to Be an Indian: When Spiritual Searching Turns into Cultural Theft," http://wantingtobeindian.bravehost.com/Wanting2BNDN1.html.

65. Ibid.

66. Smith, "For All Those Who Were Indians," 45.

67. Jeannine Hill Fletcher, *Monopoly on Salvation? A Feminist Approach to Religious Pluralism* (New York: Continuum, 2005). Hereafter reference to this book will be given in parentheses in the text.

68. For an analysis of the "self-in-relation theory" and a critique, see Marcia Westkott, "Female Relationality and the Idealized Self," *American Journal of Psychoanalysis* 49, no. 3 (1989): 239–50.

69. Johnson, "Wanting to Be an Indian."

70. Homi K. Bhabha, "Signs Taken for Wonder," in *The Location of Culture* (London: Routledge, 1994), 116.

71. Desmond Tutu, "Our Glorious Diversity: Why We Should Celebrate Difference," http://www.huffingtonpost.com/desmond-tutu/our-glorious-diversity-wh_b_874791.html.

72. "US Muslims to Remember September 11 Attacks,"

http://www.islamonline.net/en/IOLArticle_C/1278408 948377/1278406708816/IOLArticle_C.

73. Michael Kinnamon, "National Council of Churches: Worship Resources for the Ten Year Remembrance of 9/11," http://www.ncccusa.org/pdfs/911liturgy.pdf.

74. "A Litany of Remembrance, Penitence and Hope," http://www.ncccusa.org/interfaith/sept-11-litany.html.

75. Colleen Hartung, "Faith and Polydoxy in the Whirlwind," in *Polydoxy: Theology of Multiplicity and Relation*, ed. Catherine Keller and Laurel C. Schneider (London: Routledge, 2011), 153.

76. Catherine Keller and Laurel C. Schneider, "Introduction," in *Polydoxy*, 1–15.

77. Michael Hardt and Antonio Negri, *Multitude: War and Democracy in the Age of Empire* (New York: Penguin Books, 2005), xiii–xiv.

78. Laurel C. Schneider, *Beyond Monotheism: A Theology of Multiplicity* (London: Routledge, 2008), 20.

79. Ibid., 155.

80. Ibid., 155–56.

81. Ivone Gebara, *Longing for Running Water: Ecofeminism and Liberation* (Minneapolis: Fortress Press, 1999), 151–71.

82. John Thatamanil, "God as Ground, Contingency, and Relation: Trinitarian Polydoxy and Religious Diversity," in *Polydoxy*, 239.

83. Ibid., 255.

84. The following quotes are from John Thatamanil, "Binocular Religious Wisdom: Learning from Multiple Religious Participation," in *99 Brattle* blog, http://99

brattle.blogspot.com/2011/02/binocular-religious-wisdom-learning.html.

85. Marion Grau, "Signs Taken for Polydoxy in a Zulu Kraal: Creative Fiction Manifested in Missionary-Native Discourse," in *Polydoxy*, 218.

86. Kwok Pui-lan, Don Compier, and Joerg Rieger, eds., *Empire and the Christian Tradition* (Minneapolis: Fortress Press, 2007).

87. Catherine Keller, *God and Power: Counter-Apocalyptic Journeys* (Minneapolis: Fortress Press, 2005), 114.

88. See R. S. Sugirtharajah's latest work, *Exploring Postcolonial Biblical Criticism: History, Method, and Practice* (Malden, MA: Wiley-Blackwell, 2011).

89. Hyo-Dong Lee, "Interreligious Dialogue as a Politics of Recognition: A Postcolonial Rereading for Interreligious Solidarity," *Journal of Religion* 85 (2005): 563–67.

90. Franz Fanon, *Black Skin, White Masks* (New York: Grove Press, 1967).

91. Lee, "Interreligious Dialogue," 590.

92. "About Women in Black," http://www.women inblack.org/en/about.

93. "A Short History of Women in Black," http://www.womeninblack.org/en/history.

94. "Women's Interfaith Initiatives in the United States Post 9/11," http://pluralism.org /reports/view/35.

95. John L. Esposito, *Unholy War: Terror in the Name of Islam* (New York: Oxford University Press, 2003), xii.

96. Juergensmeyer, *Terror in the Mind of God*, 163.

97. Ibid., 248–89.

98. Martin Luther King, Jr., "The Power of Non-Violence," http://teachingamericanhistory.org/library/index.asp?document=1131.

99. Ibid.

100. Thich Nhat Hanh, *The Heart of Understanding: Commentaries on the Prajnaparamita Heart Sutra* (Berkeley: Parallax Press, 2009), 4.

101. Thich Nhat Hanh, *Peace Is Every Step: The Path of Mindfulness in Everyday Life* (New York: Bantam Books, 1991).

102. Thich Nhat Hanh, *Being Peace*, 2nd ed. (Berkeley: Parallax, 2005), 14.

103. The Dalai Lama, *Toward a True Kinship of Faiths: How the World's Religions Can Come Together* (New York: Doubleday, 2010).

104. Ibid., ix.

105. Ibid., xiii.

106. Ibid., 165.

107. Ibid., 167.

The Madeleva Lecture in Spirituality

This series, sponsored by the Center for Spirituality, Saint Mary's College, Notre Dame, Indiana, honors annually the woman who as president of the college inaugurated its pioneering graduate program in theology, Sister M. Madeleva, CSC.

1985
Monika K. Hellwig
Christian Women in a Troubled World

1986
Sandra M. Schneiders
Women and the Word

1987
Mary Collins
Women at Prayer

1988
Maria Harris
Women and Teaching

1989
Elizabeth Dreyer
Passionate Women: Two Medieval Mystics

1990
Joan Chittister, OSB
Job's Daughters

1991
Dolores R. Leckey
Women and Creativity

1992
Lisa Sowle Cahill
Women and Sexuality

1993
Elizabeth A. Johnson
Women, Earth, and Creator Spirit

1994
Gail Porter Mandell
Madeleva: One Woman's Life

1995
Diana L. Hayes
Hagar's Daughters

1996
Jeanette Rodriguez
Stories We Live
Cuentos Que Vivimos

1997
Mary C. Boys
Jewish-Christian Dialogue

1998
Kathleen Norris
The Quotidian Mysteries

1999
Denise Lardner Carmody
An Ideal Church: A Meditation

2000
Sandra M. Schneiders
With Oil in Their Lamps

2001
Mary Catherine Hilkert
Speaking with Authority

2002
Margaret A. Farley
Compassionate Respect

2003
Sidney Callahan
Women Who Hear Voices

2004
Mary Ann Hinsdale, IHM
Women Shaping Theology

[No Lecture in 2005]

2006
Susan A. Ross
For the Beauty of the Earth

2007
M. Shawn Copeland
The Subversive Power of Love

2008
Barbara Fiand
Awe-Filled Wonder

2009
Anne E. Patrick
Women, Conscience, and the Creative Process

2010
Wendy M. Wright
Mary and the Catholic Imagination:
Le Point Vierge